AF725302

The 24-Hour Spy Thriller with ChatGPT

Andrew Parry

Published by Andrew Parry, 2025.

While every precaution has been taken in the preparation of this book, the publisher assumes no responsibility for errors or omissions, or for damages resulting from the use of the information contained herein.

THE 24-HOUR SPY THRILLER WITH CHATGPT

First edition. May 13, 2025.

Copyright © 2025 Andrew Parry.

ISBN: 979-8231751952

Written by Andrew Parry.

Table of Contents

Writing a Spy or Political Thriller in One Day Using ChatGPT

Writing a compelling political or espionage thriller in just one day sounds like an impossible task—until you realize that your secret weapon isn't a hidden safe house or encrypted database. It's ChatGPT. With the right mindset and creative fuel, AI becomes the perfect writing partner, helping you structure, shape, and sprint through the process of crafting a high-stakes narrative full of secrets, betrayal, political maneuvering, and adrenaline-pumping action.

You don't need to spend six months plotting. You don't need to build an expansive character bible or construct fifty subplots. This isn't about perfection; it's about momentum. If you've got a few ideas, a spark of curiosity, and the willingness to work fast and stay flexible, then ChatGPT can guide you through the entire process. Think of this chapter as your classified briefing—where you learn how to deploy your digital ally to create a thrilling story before the day ends.

The first shift you have to make is realizing that you're not working alone. ChatGPT isn't just a word generator. It's a brainstorming machine, a story structure analyst, a dialogue polisher, a research assistant, and a plot trouble-shooter all rolled into one. The more clearly you communicate with it, the better the results. If you feed it an idea—no matter how rough—it will give you structure. If you describe a character—even vaguely—it will suggest flaws, motivations, relationships, and backstories. That's not just useful—it's powerful when you're writing fast.

Now, before you type a single word of your actual story, you need to define your mission. Every thriller has a mission—something the hero must do, uncover, stop, or survive. That mission is your anchor. You might have an idea like "a rogue CIA agent uncovers a conspiracy inside the UN" or "a whistleblower discovers a plot to trigger a war in Eastern Europe." It doesn't need to be polished. It just needs to be specific enough to have tension and stakes. You can throw this idea at ChatGPT and ask it to brainstorm possible plot progressions, character roles, or climaxes. Within minutes, you've got threads to follow.

Next comes your story's destination. Most people start from the beginning—but not us. We start from the end. Ask yourself: how does it all come together? Does the hero expose the truth to the world, or do they die with the secret? Does the villain win? Does the hero lose everything but manage to stop the war? When you begin with the final reveal, your narrative becomes like a reverse-engineered time bomb. Every scene you write moves your story toward a detonating truth that must come out. And when you tell ChatGPT your ending, it can map the road to get there, scene by scene.

Once your core concept and ending are roughly in place, it's time to get personal. Your story needs a protagonist—not just a spy or politician, but a person. Someone with a worldview, a weakness, a past. This is where ChatGPT really shines. You can ask it to help you build a character around a personality flaw or a professional role. Maybe your spy has PTSD from a failed mission. Maybe your political hero is corrupt but searching for redemption. Maybe your journalist is idealistic and about to be broken. You don't need to spend hours on this—ask ChatGPT to generate a character profile with specific qualities and conflicts. You can tweak it until it feels like someone you could throw into chaos.

Now your character needs something to lose. Family. Reputation. Freedom. Life. A good thriller always asks, "What's at stake?" and the more personal that stake is, the more it grips your reader. Political thrillers often intertwine personal loss with national disaster—so if your hero is trying to stop a coup, make sure someone they love is inside the blast radius. If they're a spy unraveling a conspiracy, let them discover it's connected to their past. When you give ChatGPT your hero and your ending, you can ask it to generate escalating personal and political stakes. You'll get gold.

Then comes structure. You don't need to invent your own. The three-act structure works beautifully in thrillers. Act One sets up the mission and the deception. Act Two escalates the danger and forces your hero into moral grey zones. Act Three is the confrontation, reveal, and resolution—whether victory, tragedy, or a haunting compromise. Tell ChatGPT your story, your ending, and your character, and ask it to break your idea into this three-act structure. Then, ask it to flesh out what happens in each act. You'll get a roadmap that will save you hours.

Once you've got your structure, don't stop to second-guess. Start writing. And don't worry about the opening line being perfect. You can always ask ChatGPT to improve it later. You're on a mission. Treat your writing session like a field operation—get in, complete the objective, get out. If you hit a wall, ChatGPT is there to unstick you. Can't think of how to escalate the tension in the second act? Ask. Need a fast description of a foreign capital? Ask. Need five ways your hero could escape a surveillance team in London? Ask. Don't let inertia win.

You'll be surprised how fast you can go when you lean into momentum. You can tell ChatGPT where you're at in the story and ask what should happen next. You can feed it paragraphs and ask it to punch up the dialogue or describe the scene in more visceral detail. You can even write rough drafts and ask for rewrites in a more specific voice—gritty, cinematic, noir, whatever you need.

If you're writing a short story, aim for 3,000 to 5,000 words. If you're drafting a screenplay, aim for about 90 minutes of screen time—one minute per page. If you want to write a fast-paced novel, try hitting 10,000 to 15,000 words. No matter your format, don't overthink. You're not trying to write the next *Tinker Tailor Soldier Spy* in one day. You're writing a thrilling first draft that *feels* complete. You can always polish later. Right now, it's about finishing.

In a single day, with ChatGPT in your corner, you can go from concept to climax. You can write your scenes in order or out of order. You can start with the ending, or write the action sequences first. You're not limited by linear thinking. You're free to create fast, guided by the structure and suggestions AI helps generate on the fly.

This is a new kind of writing process. One that merges creativity with acceleration. It doesn't make the story less valuable—it just means you're using modern tools to write like an elite operative. Quick. Focused. Strategic. That's how a one-day thriller gets made. And once you've done it once, you'll realize the only thing more addictive than a great spy story... is writing one yourself.

Ready to plot your operation? The next chapter takes you deeper into idea generation—with prompts and patterns to jumpstart your next espionage masterpiece.

Why Political and Espionage Thrillers Still Matter

Political and espionage thrillers have never gone out of style, and there's a reason for that. They tap into something deeper than just action or suspense. These stories give readers and viewers a front-row seat to the secret machinery of power, to the invisible wars being waged in boardrooms, backrooms, and bunkers. They reveal how fragile peace is, how layered the truth can be, and how one person's choices—often made in silence and secrecy—can change the course of history. These are not just stories of spies and politicians. They are stories about trust, betrayal, loyalty, sacrifice, and the terrifying cost of knowing too much.

What gives this genre its staying power is how it mirrors the world around us. Every decade, the political climate changes, alliances shift, new enemies emerge, and old ideologies rise again in new disguises. Espionage thrillers thrive in uncertainty. They survive on blurred lines and moral grey areas. In a world where people are constantly questioning what's true and who they can believe, these thrillers become more than entertainment—they become psychological and cultural touchstones.

Think of the Cold War era. Back then, spy thrillers were about looming nuclear threats, double agents, and iron curtains. Films like *The Spy Who Came in from the Cold* or *Dr. Strangelove* didn't just reflect paranoia—they helped people make sense of it. Fast forward to the post-9/11 world, and we see thrillers morph into something more urgent, more chaotic, more morally compromised. Stories like *Zero Dark Thirty*, *Body of Lies*, or *Homeland* took the genre into darker, messier places. It wasn't just about good versus evil anymore. It was about the price of security, the ethics of surveillance, the haunting consequences of black ops.

Even now, with global politics increasingly polarized and surveillance more sophisticated than ever, the genre is still evolving. It's not just about spies in trench coats or politicians scheming behind closed doors. It's about whistle-blowers, data theft, deepfakes, election interference, cyberattacks, and digital warfare. Today's thriller writers are grappling with a world that is simultaneously more connected and more divided, more transparent and more secretive. And readers love it. Because underneath the twists and turns is a lingering question: what if this is real?

And that question is what makes political and espionage thrillers hit so hard. When done well, they don't just entertain—they provoke thought. They make you wonder about the things you don't see on the news. About the deals that happen off-camera. About the motivations of people in power, and the quiet heroes working in the shadows to stop catastrophe. It's not just the bomb under the table that matters—it's who knew about it, who planted it, and who stood to gain.

This genre also taps into a primal fear and fascination with secrecy. As humans, we're hardwired to be curious about things we're not supposed to know. And spy thrillers dangle those secrets in front of us. They let us pretend, for a few hours, that we understand the games of power, the codes, the hidden agendas. We get to feel clever when we spot the twist, when we realize who's the mole, when we figure out what's really going on before the protagonist does. It's a genre built on tension, on quiet dread, and on the slow unfurling of truths that have massive consequences.

But it's not all just shadowy meetings and encrypted messages. At the heart of every great political or espionage thriller is a human story. A character wrestling with impossible decisions, carrying guilt, holding secrets, or trying to do the right thing in a world that punishes honesty. These thrillers are often stories of isolation. Of people who can't trust anyone. Of people whose friends might be foes, and whose enemies might be telling the truth. And that makes for deeply emotional, character-driven narratives that hit harder than any car chase or shootout ever could.

The emotional weight of these stories is what separates them from standard action fare. A political thriller might have action, but it's always layered with personal and philosophical tension. The hero might be trying to stop a war, but he's also grappling with a betrayal from someone he trusted. The spy might complete her mission, but not without losing something vital in the process—her identity, her conscience, her family. These are stories of cost. And that's what makes them resonate long after the last chapter.

Political and espionage thrillers also give writers the chance to explore enormous themes without ever sounding preachy. Through character and plot, you can explore the idea of loyalty to a flawed country, the dangers of unchecked power, the sacrifice of truth for security, the slippery slope of compromise. You can wrestle with the ethics of assassination, the justification of war, the manipulation of media. You can question whether freedom is just an illusion or whether one person really can change a system built on lies.

And because this genre so often intersects with real events, it has a built-in engine for relevance. Every time a leak is published, a politician is assassinated, a whistle-blower flees a country, or a new global conflict arises, the genre gets new fuel. Readers are paying attention because they see echoes of real life. They see things that could be happening right now—or might happen tomorrow. And they want to understand, to imagine, to feel like they're seeing behind the curtain.

That's the magic of it. Political and espionage thrillers let us play out our fears and fascinations in controlled chaos. They give us a temporary sense of understanding in a world that often feels out of our control. They let us root for the underdog, cheer for justice, or even just marvel at the intricacy of it all. And the best part? When you sit down to write one, you get to be the puppet master. You control the secrets. You decide who lives, who betrays, who wins, and what it all means in the end.

So when someone asks why political and espionage thrillers still matter, the answer is simple: because we still live in a world of secrets. We still live in a world where information is power, and where one story can expose or conceal the truth. And as long as that's true, this genre will always have something to say.

Let's move into the next step: turning those real-world anxieties and curiosities into bold, gripping story ideas—with the help of ChatGPT. That's where the fun begins.

From the End to the Beginning: Plotting Backwards for Maximum Impact

If you really want your political or espionage thriller to grip readers from page one, you have to start at the end. That might sound backwards—and that's exactly the point. In thrillers where the stakes are high and secrets are everything, the final revelation, the twist, or the outcome is what gives every earlier moment its meaning. Working backwards forces you to think like a strategist. Like a spy. Like a master manipulator of story and suspense.

A great ending doesn't just conclude a plot—it reframes everything that came before. It causes the reader to re-evaluate every scene, every piece of dialogue, every decision. That's the kind of impact we want. Whether your ending is tragic, redemptive, or morally gray, building toward it in reverse lets you drop clues with precision, escalate tension with clarity, and craft characters whose arcs lead somewhere inevitable, yet unexpected.

Let's imagine an ending together. Say your final scene is the protagonist standing alone on a snowy airstrip, watching a plane disappear into the clouds. A corrupt official escapes justice, but not before your hero made sure the secret files were leaked to the press. It's a victory, but a lonely one. The cost was trust, love, maybe even their freedom. That final moment is loaded with emotion, ambiguity, and consequence. So now ask: what had to happen for your story to get there?

The backward approach begins by defining that last image and pulling apart the events that led to it. What did the protagonist have to lose to reach that place? What choice sealed that fate? What information was uncovered in the final act that made all the difference? Who betrayed them, and when? What lie was revealed? What truth was ignored? Start writing those questions down, and your plot begins to write itself—not from a place of guesswork, but from purpose.

Now let's say you have that climactic moment—maybe it's a Senate hearing where the hero exposes a conspiracy, or a hostage exchange that goes sideways. Reverse engineer the chain of decisions, locations, character motivations, and plot twists that led to that showdown. If a betrayal is revealed, where was the first sign of it? If someone is shot or captured, when did the clock start ticking? What earlier decisions brought them to that exact pressure point?

This approach is a gift when working with ChatGPT. Once you articulate your desired ending—even vaguely—you can ask the AI to help you break it down into key events that logically build up to that moment. You can say, "I want the story to end with the protagonist being arrested for treason after they expose the President's private spy network—help me map out the plot backwards." And you'll get a structure that helps every single scene earn its place.

Plotting backwards also helps avoid one of the worst sins in thriller writing: meandering plots that lose focus. If you write forward without a destination, your story can drift. It might get bloated with scenes that feel dramatic but don't serve a larger arc. Starting from the end gives every decision more weight. You can foreshadow with intention. You can mislead your readers without lying to them. You're not just writing a story—you're engineering a conspiracy.

Character arcs benefit too. When you know where your hero ends up, you can trace the emotional path that gets them there. If they start out idealistic and end up disillusioned, what scenes chip away at their belief system? If they're hardened at the beginning but sacrifice themselves in the end, what relationships softened them? Plotting backwards allows you to chart that transformation beat by beat, creating characters who evolve in sync with the story, not just alongside it.

The same applies to your antagonist. If you know how the villain is revealed, defeated, or even walks away unpunished, you can plant their manipulations earlier with greater finesse. You can make them two steps ahead instead of conveniently wicked. You can build rivalries, twisted mentorships, secret alliances, and dramatic turnarounds that feel like they've been part of the story since the first page—because you wove them in with the ending already in mind.

Pacing improves, too. You can decide where the midpoint twist needs to land, where the big reveal should happen, where the characters should feel like all is lost, and where the final confrontation will occur. Plotting in reverse sets the tempo for your thriller like a conductor building toward a crashing finale. You know when to speed things up, when to slow things down, and when to blindside your reader.

Even theme works better this way. If your story is ultimately about corruption and sacrifice, you can echo those ideas earlier in subtle ways. Maybe your hero watches someone else turn a blind eye in the first act, or maybe they make a decision they'll later regret. These thematic breadcrumbs only matter if they lead somewhere. When you know what message you're ending with, you can infuse that message into every choice and subplot.

And of course, reverse plotting makes twists stronger. If your story hinges on a reveal—that someone was a mole, that a death was faked, that the government funded the very terrorists your hero's been hunting—then going backwards ensures that twist is supported. You can lay clues, misdirect the reader, and then deliver the twist in a way that makes them gasp, not groan. ChatGPT can help with that, too. You can ask it to generate scenes that foreshadow your twist without giving it away, or ask it to check if the reveal holds up under scrutiny.

There's another benefit: confidence. Writing can be daunting when you're not sure where you're headed. But when you know the last page, every page before it has direction. You're not just typing words. You're building tension toward something you've already envisioned. You're laying tracks toward a destination you've already mapped. That confidence makes it easier to write fast, which is essential when you're trying to draft a complete story in one day.

So before you open your document and start describing a dimly lit embassy or a code-breaking session in a basement, pause. Picture the end. Who's alive? Who's broken? What's changed? What's the price your hero has paid—and was it worth it? Once you know that, start climbing backward, one revelation at a time. That's how you craft a political or spy thriller that doesn't just thrill, but leaves a mark.

In the next chapter, we'll get to the fun part—how to generate dozens of gripping ideas using ChatGPT, so you never run out of missions, conspiracies, or secret wars to explore.

Generating High-Stakes Ideas with ChatGPT's Help

The secret to writing a great political or espionage thriller isn't always starting with a brilliant idea—it's knowing how to develop and escalate a small idea until it feels like the world is about to explode. High-stakes stories don't begin with explosions. They begin with tension. A buried file. A whispered name. A coded message. A small action with enormous consequences. And when you're writing fast—especially within a single day—you need to generate those high-stakes ideas quickly, and refine them just as fast. That's where ChatGPT becomes your silent partner in the shadows.

Every story starts with a question. What if? That's the gateway. And the best political and espionage thrillers ask questions that strike at the core of global stability, national identity, personal morality, or technological dominance. What if a newly elected president was a foreign asset? What if a spy discovered their mission would trigger a global war? What if a journalist was the only person who had the truth, and everyone wanted them dead? The question should raise eyebrows. It should suggest power, danger, and secrecy. That's your ignition point.

If you don't already have that question in mind, ChatGPT can help you find it. You can start by feeding it just one sentence: "Give me five high-stakes thriller ideas involving espionage and politics." You'll instantly get scenarios that include arms deals, rogue agents, hacked elections, international blackmail, or stolen nuclear codes. You can go broader or more specific. Ask for ideas set in the Middle East, or Washington, D.C., or inside a fictional fascist government. Ask for stories involving whistleblowers, corporate sabotage, military coups, or traitors in intelligence agencies.

But the trick isn't just generating ideas. It's recognizing when an idea has teeth. A good thriller idea isn't just surprising—it's volatile. It makes the reader feel that something is at stake from the very beginning. That someone's about to lose something big. That the truth could destroy everything. So when you read through a batch of ideas, ask yourself: What's the danger? Who stands to lose? What's being covered up? The stronger the answers, the stronger the premise.

You can also use ChatGPT to evolve a simple idea into something more layered. Let's say you start with: "A cyberterrorist threatens to leak government secrets unless a political prisoner is released." On its own, not bad. But now ask ChatGPT to deepen it. Who is the prisoner, and what makes them important? What secrets could be leaked, and how would their exposure disrupt global relations? What personal connection does the hero have to either side? You'll suddenly have layers of conflict, emotional stakes, and moral ambiguity. That's where the thriller lives.

Themes are also a great entry point for idea generation. If you want to write a story about surveillance, ask ChatGPT for five thriller plots where governments spy on their own citizens. If you want to tackle corruption, ask for plots involving deep-state operatives manipulating policy. If you want to explore loyalty and betrayal, ask for stories about double agents or mole hunts. You can even ask it to give you a plot where the antagonist is morally justified—and then build a hero who sees the world differently.

Once you've got an idea that crackles, start working backward from the climax, just like we covered in the last chapter. Share the core idea with ChatGPT and say, "Help me build a story around this ending." The AI can then suggest a three-act structure or a sequence of events that escalate the tension. Don't be afraid to try different variations. One of the most useful tactics is to say, "Give me five alternate endings for this story idea." Suddenly, your one premise can spawn five different thrillers.

Here's where things really get powerful: ChatGPT doesn't just give you ideas. It gives you the *worlds* around them. Ask it to describe the political climate. Ask it to create fictional countries, rogue agencies, or alliances on the brink of collapse. Ask it for realistic motives behind a secret war or intelligence operation. It will paint the background that makes your plot believable and compelling. It helps you fake expertise fast, which is critical when you're writing a thriller with global implications in one day.

And don't ignore the "character-first" approach. Sometimes the best stories start not with a plot, but with a compelling person. Ask ChatGPT to create a character who works for the CIA but secretly feeds intel to an activist group. Or someone running for office while hiding a deadly past as a covert operative. Build the character first, then ask, "What kind of story would force this person to the edge?" The character becomes the detonator that drives the plot.

You can also mix and match. Take one character from one prompt, and drop them into another plot. Take a political setting and overlay it with an espionage mission. Ask ChatGPT to blend two different thriller tropes together. "Give me a story that combines a spy thriller with a political scandal." You'll often get strange but thrilling hybrids—like an undercover agent who becomes a press secretary to cover up an assassination plot, or a diplomat who's also an arms dealer.

The other key is to not get stuck on perfection. When you're trying to write fast, the goal is momentum, not masterpieces. Don't wait for the perfect idea to strike. Generate five, choose one, and move. If it falters later, switch tracks. Ask ChatGPT, "What's a twist that could save this story at the midpoint?" or "What's a more dangerous version of this scenario?" Use the AI to keep moving forward rather than second-guessing every choice.

In a way, generating high-stakes ideas with ChatGPT is like running an operation. You're not relying on one source—you're gathering intelligence, testing angles, planting scenarios, and watching what comes alive. You're not bound to just one version of the truth. You're playing with reality, and seeing which version blows up best.

So when you're staring at a blank page and the clock is ticking, don't panic. Open a chat, ask the right questions, and let the responses light a fire under your imagination. There's always another scandal, another covert plot, another ticking clock just waiting to be written.

Next, we'll break down how to define your thriller's subgenre—because not all espionage and political thrillers are created equal, and your tone, structure, and character choices will change depending on which type of story you're telling.

Choosing Your Genre: Political Conspiracy or Espionage Action

Before you write a single line of dialogue or map out a single mission, you need to answer one simple but crucial question: what kind of thriller are you actually writing? Is this a political conspiracy, slow-burning and paranoid? Or is it an espionage action thriller, fast-paced and explosive? Both genres fall under the same shadowy umbrella, but they move at different speeds, they hit different emotional notes, and they ask different things of both the characters and the audience.

Political thrillers tend to be cerebral, layered, and morally complex. These stories unfold like a chess game between people in power—government officials, whistleblowers, activists, corporate giants, or the media. The weapon of choice isn't a gun—it's information. A leak. A secret. A deal made in silence that changes the course of a nation. The tension doesn't come from physical danger so much as intellectual threat. These stories ask: What happens when the system is the villain? What if the enemy is inside the government, inside the law, or inside the hero's own ideology?

Think of films like *All the President's Men*, *The Parallax View*, *Michael Clayton*, or even *The Ides of March*. These are not stories where bullets fly every five minutes. They're stories where every phone call could end a career, every handshake could start a war. The stakes are massive, but the pacing is slow-burn. The tension builds through discoveries, betrayals, and revelations. When you're writing a political conspiracy thriller, you're not just telling a story—you're exposing a system. The thrills are in the truth, in the lies people tell to protect their power, and in the gray areas your protagonist is forced to navigate.

Espionage action thrillers, on the other hand, are about movement, deception, and survival. These are stories where your protagonist is on the run, in disguise, dodging bullets, disarming bombs, stealing intel, or infiltrating secret compounds. The pace is fast, the action is constant, and the twists are sharper. Think *The Bourne Identity*, *Mission: Impossible*, *Jack Ryan*, *Atomic Blonde*, or *The Spy Who Came in from the Cold*—which even with its slower tone, still lives and breathes espionage danger.

In this world, trust is rare and death is always one wrong step away. Your protagonist might be a government agent, an assassin, a mole, a hacker, or a freelance operative caught between powers. The story beats harder and faster. It's physical. You need gadgets, disguises, secret rendezvous, and breathtaking escapes. But beneath all that action, there still needs to be a pulse of emotional stakes and moral ambiguity—because a great espionage thriller isn't just about what's happening, but about why it matters to the person doing it.

Now here's where it gets interesting: you don't have to choose just one lane. Many of the best thrillers blur the lines between political intrigue and spy action. You can start with a slow-burn political mystery and let it explode into a high-stakes pursuit. You can have an operative uncovering a conspiracy while dodging kill teams in foreign cities. The key is balance. Know your base genre, and then decide how much of the other you want to fold in.

This is something ChatGPT can help with in spades. You can ask it to reimagine your story idea in either genre. Say you have an idea about a missing senator. Ask ChatGPT to turn it into a political thriller, and it might suggest a journalist digging up a conspiracy involving government surveillance. Ask it to turn it into an espionage action thriller, and it might pitch a CIA agent chasing a rogue operative across Europe to recover classified documents that implicate the senator in a coup. Same core idea—completely different rhythm, tone, and structure.

So how do you decide which genre you're writing? Start by asking yourself what kind of tension you love most. Do you enjoy stories that make your heart race or stories that make your mind spiral? Are you more excited by a rooftop chase scene or a moment where a character realizes the person they trust most is lying to them? Do you want to blow something up—or uncover something quietly devastating?

Also think about your protagonist. A political thriller often features someone outside the traditional action hero role—a reporter, a lawyer, a senator, an advisor. Someone whose power is in what they know, not how they fight. An espionage thriller usually stars someone trained for this—an agent, a spy, an analyst, or a soldier with secrets. The skillset defines the genre's tone. If your character is trained in combat, surveillance, and stealth, your story will probably lean toward espionage action. If they're trained in persuasion, law, or navigating bureaucracies, you're leaning into political drama.

One of the most useful things you can do when you're still undecided is to ask ChatGPT to help you test the genre. Feed it your protagonist, setting, and stakes, and say, "Show me how this story plays out as a political thriller." Then, "Show me how it plays out as an espionage thriller." You'll quickly see which one feels more exciting to write—and which version gives your story more urgency and emotion.

There's also audience expectation to consider. Readers who pick up a spy thriller expect action, deception, and danger around every corner. Readers looking for a political thriller want something that feels grounded, even if it's fictional. They want characters who navigate power structures, who take risks by asking the wrong questions or digging into forbidden knowledge. Matching your tone to your genre isn't about following rules—it's about making sure the reader gets the experience they showed up for.

And remember, genre isn't a cage—it's a compass. It gives you direction, not limitations. Knowing whether you're in the realm of conspiracy or covert ops helps you choose your beats, structure your tension, and shape your characters. But you can still surprise your readers. You can still cross lines and blur boundaries. Just make sure the heart of your story—whether it's a man on the run or a system on the edge of collapse—beats strong.

In the next chapter, we'll dive into how to create the perfect hero for this kind of story—the kind of protagonist who's smart, flawed, capable, and compelling enough to carry the weight of a world full of lies. Whether your hero is a politician, a field agent, or someone caught in the middle, they'll need to stand tall in the shadowy world you're about to throw them into.

Creating the Perfect Hero for the Shadows

Writing a political or espionage thriller is like playing a game of high-stakes chess in the dark. Every character is a piece, every move matters, and the one holding it all together is your hero. But this isn't your typical action-movie protagonist. This hero is built for shadows. They operate in moral fog. They carry secrets like weapons. They often stand alone, bruised by the cost of knowing too much and trusting too little. To keep your story gripping, this isn't just the person who saves the world—this is the person who *survives* it, and who just might lose themselves in the process.

The perfect hero for a political or espionage thriller isn't a superhuman. They're capable, yes, but not invincible. They think fast, adapt faster, and carry a past that haunts every decision. The best ones have a contradiction at their core. Maybe they're a patriot who's beginning to doubt their country. Maybe they're a trained killer trying to live a normal life. Maybe they're a true believer forced to face the corruption of their ideals. What makes these heroes work is the tension between who they are and what they've become—between the mission and the soul.

This kind of character doesn't arrive fully formed. You build them. And with ChatGPT at your side, you can do it quickly and deeply. Start by defining their current role. Are they a spy? A political advisor? A whistleblower? A rogue agent? A war veteran turned analyst? Then ask: why are *they* the one who has to walk through the fire in this story? Why not someone else? What unique skills, knowledge, or guilt makes them the perfect target—or the perfect threat—to the world you're creating?

You can tell ChatGPT something like, "I want a protagonist who used to work for military intelligence but now runs a bookstore and gets dragged back into the world." And you'll get a character sketch—background, psychological profile, potential flaws, and strengths. From there, you shape it. What broke them? What motivates them now? What's the thing they swore they'd never do again—but will be forced to do by page 100?

Your hero in a thriller needs one thing above all: agency. They must *act*, not just react. They can start as a pawn, but they should evolve into a player. Maybe they start off following orders or trying to escape danger, but by the midpoint of your story, they're making their own plays, pulling their own strings, taking risks nobody else would. You want a character who surprises even themselves. Someone who's not just capable of violence, but capable of making the impossible decision—and living with the cost.

That cost is everything in this genre. The hero almost always sacrifices something. Peace of mind. A relationship. Their reputation. Their safety. Sometimes their life. A great political or espionage thriller isn't about a perfect win—it's about what's lost in the process of saving what matters. So give your hero something worth protecting, and something they're terrified to lose. It could be a daughter, a partner, a memory, an ideal, or even a secret they've kept buried for years. When your hero's motivation is personal, the stakes are never just global—they're intimate.

Don't forget about flaws. Nobody wants to follow a spotless operative who always makes the right call. Give your hero regrets. Maybe they left someone behind. Maybe they obeyed a terrible order and can't forgive themselves. Maybe they're still hiding something from everyone—including the reader. These flaws humanize them, make them unpredictable, and give you moments of inner conflict that mirror the external chaos. Use ChatGPT to suggest conflicting personality traits, or ask for ways to make your hero's weakness become their strength—or vice versa.

Another thing that defines your hero is how they navigate truth. In a thriller built around lies, manipulation, and shifting alliances, your protagonist needs a personal compass. That doesn't mean they always tell the truth—but they have a line they won't cross. At least at first. The tension in many espionage heroes is how far they'll go before the mission destroys who they were trying to be. Will they kill? Will they lie to someone they love? Will they trade one life for a hundred? These questions *are* the story. Don't just write them into your plot—bake them into your character.

And then there's the mask. In this genre, identity is fluid. Your hero might be pretending to be someone else. Or they might be someone else pretending to be who they used to be. That duality gives you so much to play with. You can write scenes where the hero's cover nearly slips, where they reveal too much, or where they don't even know who they are anymore. Ask ChatGPT to help you create a double life—one public, one private—and see where the tension lies between the two.

Your hero also needs someone to push against. Not just an enemy, but a reflection of what they could become. Your antagonist—whether it's a corrupt politician, a rival spy, a manipulative agency head, or a traitor within—should challenge your hero's beliefs. They might even *agree* with your hero's motives, but not their methods. Or vice versa. The more personal the connection between hero and antagonist, the sharper your story becomes.

Now, when you're writing a story in one day, you can't afford to spend three hours building a backstory. But that's where ChatGPT becomes essential. Ask it for your character's five defining moments. Ask for three traumatic memories and how they shaped their personality. Ask for a code of conduct they live by—and a scenario that would make them break it. These prompts generate rich internal terrain for your character, even if your plot is racing across continents.

Remember: in this genre, your hero's biggest enemy isn't always the assassin down the hall. Sometimes it's the weight of past decisions. Sometimes it's the truth they don't want to face. The perfect hero for the shadows doesn't just shine light into the world's darkest corners—they also shine it on themselves. And what they find there isn't always pretty.

In the next chapter, we'll dive deep into the construction of your story's villain—because in this genre, the antagonist isn't just a bad guy. They're the one pulling strings, rewriting rules, and threatening everything your hero thought was real.

Building a Villain with Real Power and Hidden Motives

In a political or espionage thriller, the villain isn't just some maniac waving a gun or blowing up a building for fun. That might work in a popcorn action flick, but if you want to write a story with staying power—something that feels dangerous, chilling, and plausible—you need an antagonist who is terrifying because of what they know, what they control, and what they're willing to sacrifice to achieve their goal. A great villain in this genre is a puppeteer, a strategist, a ghost in the machine. They rarely shout. They smile. And they always think they're right.

Your hero lives in the shadows, but your villain *owns* the shadows. They built the system the hero is trying to dismantle. They have real power—political, financial, military, or psychological. That power isn't always flashy. It might be a signature on a bill that authorizes secret surveillance. It might be control over the media narrative. It might be silence in a committee room that covers up a war crime. This kind of power is scary not because it's loud, but because it's invisible to everyone except your protagonist.

The first thing you need to decide is this: what does your villain want, and why? It's not enough to say they want power. Everyone in a political thriller wants power. That's just the starting line. What makes your villain compelling is how they define power—and what they're willing to do to get it. Maybe they believe peace can only be achieved through total control. Maybe they want to protect their country by any means necessary. Maybe they're a true believer in a cause that justifies bloodshed. Or maybe they just want to burn it all down to build something new.

One of the most unsettling truths in this genre is that the villain doesn't always see themselves as a villain. In fact, they often think they're the only one who sees the big picture. They're logical. Calculated. They're doing what needs to be done, while everyone else is too scared or too soft to make the hard choices. That's what makes them dangerous—they believe in something. That belief can come from trauma, ideology, revenge, or even love. Ask ChatGPT to explore different motives based on a few key facts about your antagonist, and you'll get a palette of compelling possibilities.

Don't make your villain too obvious. In espionage and political thrillers, the real villain often wears a smile and shakes hands with presidents. They might be a senator who gives patriotic speeches while secretly orchestrating assassinations. A corporate CEO funding both sides of a war. A spymaster who's been playing the long game for decades. The deeper their roots in the system, the more impossible they seem to defeat. The reader should get that creeping sense that the villain's influence is everywhere, even when they're off the page.

And when they *are* on the page, make it count. Their presence should shift the energy of a scene. They don't have to yell or throw threats around. They can be calm, charming, maybe even likable. That's what makes them harder to pin down. The scariest villain is the one who makes you question your own side. Who makes the reader pause and think, "Wait... maybe they have a point." You want moral complexity, not cartoonish evil. Let them talk about philosophy, not just tactics. Let them seduce the audience intellectually before they strike.

Use ChatGPT to build the backstory for your villain with the same care as your protagonist. Ask it to develop a five-stage evolution of how they became the person they are. Ask what trauma shaped their worldview. What mentor twisted their values. What belief hardened into obsession. Maybe they were once a hero. Maybe they served with honor, only to watch everything they believed in get corrupted. Maybe they were betrayed by the very system they now seek to control. The more layered their story, the more powerful their presence.

Another essential element is secrecy. Your villain should have motives that aren't clear until the second or third act. They should have goals behind goals. A fake mission that distracts the hero from the real one. A partnership that turns out to be a trap. A betrayal that goes deeper than anyone guessed. Ask ChatGPT to give you five hidden motives that would make sense for your villain based on the plot you've built so far. Then start layering those into scenes—maybe as hints, maybe as contradictions in their behavior, maybe as a reveal from a secondary character who used to trust them.

And don't forget how your villain relates to your hero. The best antagonists are reflections of the protagonist's fears or flaws. If your hero values transparency, let the villain weaponize secrecy. If your hero believes in saving lives, let the villain justify sacrifices. If your hero lost someone to betrayal, let the villain exploit that wound. This isn't just about creating conflict—it's about creating emotional pressure. The villain should challenge your hero in ways that force growth, force doubt, force transformation.

Finally, your villain needs an exit. Maybe they die. Maybe they disappear. Maybe they win. But whatever their fate, make it meaningful. Their downfall (or triumph) should feel earned. If they fall, it should be because of the one thing they didn't see coming—whether it's a flaw in their logic, a betrayal from an ally, or a moment of human weakness. If they survive, it should feel like the story's world has truly changed. Use ChatGPT to help you generate potential endings for your villain—some satisfying, some disturbing, all plausible. That way, you're never boxed in.

Writing a political or espionage thriller without a compelling villain is like sending your hero into a warzone without an enemy. It's the villain who gives the story shape, direction, and gravity. Build them not just as an obstacle, but as a force of nature. Make them smart, motivated, patient, and terrifying in their precision. Let them wear a human face, speak calmly, and make the reader wonder if the world wouldn't be better off if they won.

Next up, we'll take a look at how to create dual identities—because in this genre, nothing is what it seems, and everyone's wearing a mask. Including your hero.

The Double Life: Giving Your Characters Dual Realities

In the world of political and espionage thrillers, nobody is just one thing. The operative isn't just an operative—they're a husband, a mother, a mentor, or a recovering addict. The senator isn't just a public servant—they're a dealmaker in back rooms, a protector of dark secrets, or a cog in a machine they can't stop. The journalist exposing the conspiracy? They might be compromised, or worse, secretly working for the people they claim to be exposing. In this genre, double lives aren't just common—they're essential.

Every compelling character in your story should carry the weight of two realities. One is public. The other is private. One is the identity the world sees. The other is the identity that navigates shadows, answers to other masters, or guards truths too dangerous to speak aloud. When you build a character with a dual reality, you open the door to deeper conflict, richer drama, and the kind of tension that makes a thriller impossible to put down.

Let's start with your protagonist. Maybe they're a diplomat with access to global leaders and a closet full of perfectly tailored suits. But when the lights go down, they pass information to a rogue intelligence faction. Or maybe your hero is an investigative reporter who appears obsessed with the truth—but in private, they're burying a secret that would destroy their credibility. The contrast between who they are and who they pretend to be is what creates emotional pressure. It forces them to compartmentalize, lie, and navigate situations where revealing their true self could get them killed—or worse.

Dual identities also allow for incredible storytelling tension. Every conversation becomes a performance. Every scene has subtext. A character might say one thing and mean another. A friendly dinner could be a subtle interrogation. A romantic moment could be a test of loyalty. The reader always wonders: who really knows the truth? Who is playing who? That ambiguity is rocket fuel for suspense.

You can use ChatGPT to generate detailed double-life concepts for any character. Let's say you want a secondary character to have a hidden agenda. Ask the AI: "Give me a background for a senator who is secretly leaking intel to a foreign power but genuinely believes they're protecting democracy." You'll get motivations, contradictions, possible scenes of internal conflict, and even ways they might slip or reveal their true allegiance. You can do this for protagonists, antagonists, or anyone in between.

But don't stop at the lie itself. What matters more is *why* they're living it. Are they protecting someone? Do they believe their lie serves a greater good? Were they coerced into a second identity and now can't escape? Maybe they were idealists who lost faith and now live in a constant state of cognitive dissonance. This genre is built on characters who are trapped in moral mazes—and the dual life is the perfect way to express that.

The double life also gives you room to show how deception bleeds into everything. A spy who lies for a living can start to lose the ability to be truthful even in safe spaces. A politician who bends reality to fit public narratives might do the same in their personal life, unable to tell their family what's really happening. That internal erosion is compelling to watch. It gives you quiet, human moments between the explosions and chase scenes. It's what makes the genre resonate.

One way to structure a dual-life character is to give them a "cover identity," a "true identity," and a "conflicted identity." The cover identity is who they pretend to be. The true identity is who they were trained or forced to become. And the conflicted identity is who they wish they could be if they weren't stuck in the game. You can sketch this out with

ChatGPT quickly by prompting, "Describe a CIA agent with these three versions of self." The result gives you material for internal monologues, conflicting actions, and character evolution throughout the story.

And don't forget the dramatic potential of a dual life being exposed. That moment where the mask slips—on purpose or by accident—is often the most intense scene in the whole story. Maybe someone recognizes them at a gala. Maybe an encrypted message goes to the wrong inbox. Maybe a child finds a hidden passport and asks a question the character can't answer. Exposure equals danger. But it also equals truth. And sometimes, that moment of truth becomes the turning point of the whole narrative.

Dual lives aren't just for heroes either. Your villain might also be living one. They might be admired in public and monstrous in private. Or they might be deeply misunderstood, acting as a villain in one world and a reluctant saviour in another. Some of the best antagonists are those whose dual lives mirror the hero's, forcing them to confront their own choices in a twisted reflection.

Romantic subplots also get more intense with dual identities in play. How can your protagonist fall in love when everything about them is a lie? How do they confess who they really are without endangering the person they care about? Or what if the person they're falling for is also playing a part? Suddenly, the relationship becomes a psychological minefield. Trust, betrayal, longing, and danger all wrapped into one volatile package.

Dual lives give your story fuel. They allow for misdirection, twist reveals, inner conflict, emotional stakes, and the kind of scenes where someone is smiling and joking—while holding a knife behind their back. It's not about tricking the reader for the sake of surprise. It's about showing that in this world, truth is a luxury, and survival often means pretending to be someone you're not.

Protagonists Who Carry Secrets and Scars

Every protagonist in a political or espionage thriller is hiding something. Sometimes it's a classified piece of intel. Sometimes it's a mistake they swore never to repeat. Sometimes it's a truth about themselves they can't even admit out loud. These are not clean-slate heroes. They're people stitched together with trauma, lies, loyalty, and guilt. They walk into every scene with a little less innocence, and they carry their emotional and psychological baggage like an unmarked briefcase they dare not open.

If you want your story to hit with emotional weight—not just adrenaline—you need a protagonist who feels real beneath the bullets and conspiracies. And real people carry scars. Some are physical. Most are not. These scars are what fuel the inner journey of your hero while they navigate the chaos of the external plot. They're what make your character hesitate when they should act, or go too far when they should hold back. They create tension not just between characters, but within your protagonist's own mind.

Let's start with the kind of secrets that define this genre. The most common—and most effective—are the ones that could change everything if exposed. Maybe your hero once committed a war crime under orders and it's been buried ever since. Maybe they're the only one who knows a mole's identity, but revealing it would cost someone close to them their life. Maybe they're hiding their real name, their real past, or their real allegiance. These aren't just plot devices. These secrets shape how your character sees the world and interacts with everyone in it.

And then there are emotional secrets. Maybe your protagonist lost someone in an operation gone wrong and blames themselves. Maybe they were betrayed by someone they trusted—someone who's back in their life now, on the other side of the mission. Maybe they're holding onto a belief that no longer fits the world they live in. Emotional secrets don't have to be huge—they just have to be heavy. They create internal tension that mirrors the external stakes, and they give you room to create moments of silence, regret, and doubt between the chaos.

Ask ChatGPT to help you generate a secret based on your protagonist's role, background, and goals. A prompt like, "Give me a secret for a former NSA analyst turned whistle-blower that could destroy them if revealed" can result in options that you can thread through your plot. The secret doesn't need to be dumped into the story all at once. Let it simmer. Hint at it. Let it bleed into their decisions, their reactions, the people they avoid or protect. Let it be something the reader discovers gradually.

Scars, on the other hand, are what's left after the secret has done its damage. These scars can be mental, emotional, physical, or behavioral. A protagonist might have PTSD from a past mission. Maybe they're addicted to adrenaline, pills, or the rush of danger because it's the only thing that drowns the noise in their head. Maybe they're emotionally shut down, unable to connect with anyone unless they're under threat. These aren't clichés—they're reflections of what this kind of life costs. Use ChatGPT to ask, "What psychological effects would a covert operative suffer after ten years of black ops missions?" and you'll get a realistic foundation to build your hero's inner world.

What makes these secrets and scars powerful is when they interfere with the mission. When the hero can't pull the trigger because of what happened last time. When they trust the wrong person because they miss someone they lost. When they sabotage their own success out of guilt or shame. The inner conflict should echo and complicate the outer one. It doesn't make your protagonist weaker—it makes them human.

Another key is to use these hidden wounds to shape relationships. If your hero has a partner, a handler, a love interest, or even an enemy, those interactions should be laced with subtext. The reader should sense there's something unspoken beneath every conversation. A tension. A hesitation. A past. This is where dialogue becomes a tool for both misdirection and revelation. Let your characters speak in coded emotional language. Let one line of dialogue carry five meanings. That's the kind of writing that makes a thriller emotionally rich instead of just technically sharp.

It's also worth noting that not all secrets and scars have to come from violence or trauma. Some of the most effective come from moments of moral failure. Maybe your hero betrayed a cause they believed in. Maybe they once manipulated someone for an op and still carry that shame. Maybe they turned a blind eye to injustice and now can't look at themselves in the mirror. These are the kinds of wounds that don't leave a mark on the body—but cut deeper than anything else.

And here's the thing: your hero doesn't have to resolve every scar by the end. In fact, sometimes it's more honest if they don't. Growth can be messy. Maybe they confess their secret and still lose everything. Maybe they overcome the fear—but not the guilt. Maybe they win the war and walk away lonelier than when it began. That's the cost of carrying secrets. That's the reality of being someone who operates in shadows. You can save the world and still lose something inside yourself.

Use ChatGPT to build moments of emotional unraveling. Ask for a scene where the protagonist almost confesses their secret but pulls back. Or one where a minor character sees through the mask. Or one where the scar becomes a strength just long enough to survive the next twist. These small, personal moments will matter just as much as the big action beats.

A protagonist who carries secrets and scars becomes the soul of your story. They're not just reacting to external threats—they're navigating an internal minefield. They're trying to do the right thing with broken tools. And that makes every choice they make feel like it could tip the balance between salvation and self-destruction.

In the next chapter, we'll take a turn toward the enemy's side—exploring how to write antagonists who believe they're the real heroes. Because sometimes the only difference between the hero and the villain is which secret they chose to carry—and which one they chose to reveal.

Antagonists who think they're the Hero

In the world of political and espionage thrillers, villains aren't always obvious. They don't walk around twirling moustaches or delivering dramatic speeches from war rooms. The most compelling antagonists in this genre are those who look in the mirror and see a savior. They believe they're right. They believe their actions—however dark, brutal, or unethical—are for the greater good. And they're not just pretending. They *believe*. That belief is what makes them dangerous.

If your antagonist is convinced they're the good guy, the story takes on a layered complexity that elevates every scene. Suddenly, your hero isn't just facing off against someone evil—they're facing someone principled. Someone driven. Someone with a mission. When the antagonist truly believes in their cause, they become more than a threat. They become a reflection of what your hero *could* become under different circumstances.

Start by asking yourself a simple question: what does your antagonist want, and why do they believe it's necessary? Maybe they want to destabilize a corrupt regime. Maybe they want to reveal government secrets that would cause chaos but also accountability. Maybe they want to kill a leader to prevent a war. The act may be horrific, but the *intention* behind it is what makes the character complex. You don't have to agree with them—but the audience should understand them.

Ask ChatGPT to help develop an antagonist who believes they are saving lives, or protecting freedom, or fixing a broken system. A great prompt might be: "Create an antagonist who is trying to prevent a nuclear conflict by starting a controlled cyber war." You'll get motivations, strategies, and personal philosophies that make the character feel grounded in something real. Once you have their "why," every decision they make can stem from that belief.

Now let's give them a moral code. It doesn't have to be the same as the hero's—it might be stricter, or colder, or more utilitarian. Maybe your antagonist won't kill innocents, but will gladly ruin reputations. Maybe they see death as a mathematical necessity. Or maybe they believe that lying is justified if it reveals a deeper truth. The point is, they operate by *rules*. They're not chaotic. They're not evil for the sake of drama. They are logical, methodical, and terrifyingly consistent.

And it gets better when you explore how this moral code collides with your protagonist. If your hero is trying to stop a war through diplomacy, and your antagonist is trying to start a war to reset the global balance, you've got ideological tension. You've got dialogue that bites, not because it's angry, but because it's *convincing*. The best villain scenes are the ones where the hero is shaken—not by a threat, but by the possibility that the villain is *right*.

This kind of antagonist doesn't even have to be secretive. In fact, sometimes they're more chilling when they're transparent. A politician on camera declaring their intent to "cleanse the system," or an ex-intelligence officer calmly explaining that the only way to prevent collapse is to trigger controlled chaos. These are the kinds of characters that haunt you because they don't flinch. They don't yell. They don't gloat. They state their beliefs clearly—and dare the world to stop them.

Of course, many of these antagonists have scars of their own. They weren't born this way. Something shaped them. Maybe it was betrayal by the system they once served. Maybe they lost someone and swore it would never happen again. Maybe they were heroes once—before the truth broke them. You can use ChatGPT to build a past that explains their present. Ask for defining moments, failed missions, or personal losses that pushed them into the role of antagonist. These moments will help you write scenes where their pain comes through, even as they commit unforgivable acts.

And don't forget: sometimes they're *not* wrong. Maybe the government *is* corrupt. Maybe the truth *should* be revealed. Maybe the hero, in trying to stop them, is actually maintaining a status quo that needs to fall. That kind of moral ambiguity is the heartbeat of a good thriller. It forces the reader to keep asking: who deserves to win?

The interactions between your hero and villain become electric when they both believe they're doing the right thing. They can sit across a table and talk instead of fight—and the tension is unbearable. They can argue ideologies, accuse each other of hypocrisy, and reveal truths that neither one is ready to face. These scenes don't need explosions. They need silence, eye contact, and a slow dawning realization that they might not be so different after all.

You can also flip this dynamic midway through the story. Let the hero discover that the villain used to be just like them. Let the antagonist try to recruit the hero. Let them offer a seat at the table. Let them say, "I was where you are once. Until I saw what the world really is." If your protagonist hesitates—even for a second—you've added weight to their arc. That hesitation is everything. It shows that the villain didn't just threaten them physically—they got into their head.

And when it comes to endings, these kinds of villains don't always have to die. Sometimes they escape. Sometimes they go to prison and still smile as the hero walks away. Sometimes they *win*, and the hero is left questioning everything. Ask ChatGPT to suggest endings for morally complex villains—some satisfying, some disturbing, and all shaped by ideology. The right ending should echo the themes of your story: truth, loyalty, sacrifice, deception.

A great antagonist in this genre doesn't just drive the plot. They shape the world. They force your hero to evolve. They blur the lines. And when they walk off the page, they leave you thinking, "Would I have done the same thing?"

In the next chapter, we'll explore how to start the story in motion—those opening scenes where the reader is thrown into danger, deception, or discovery from the very first line. Because in the world of espionage and politics, the hook has to cut deep, and fast.

Laying the Groundwork: Where the Mission Starts

In a political or espionage thriller, the mission is never just a mission. It's the thread that, when pulled, unravels an entire world of secrets. But before the guns come out, before the surveillance teams move into place, before the betrayals begin to drop like dominoes, there's a moment where everything seems calm—almost too calm. That's where your story starts. Right there, on the edge of the storm. And getting that beginning right is everything.

The first act of your thriller is about laying groundwork. Not dumping exposition or overwhelming the reader with backstory—but establishing the tone, the world, the stakes, and the first crack in the façade. It's the moment when the hero's ordinary world—whatever they've been pretending is normal—is disrupted by something they can't ignore. That disruption doesn't need to be loud. It can be subtle. A coded message. A suspicious glance. A name that shouldn't be on a list. A story that's just a little too clean. In this genre, the mission rarely kicks off with a bang. It starts with a whisper.

One of the first questions you should ask as a writer is: *Where is my protagonist when the story begins—and what are they trying to ignore?* That's usually where the best inciting incidents hide. Maybe they've retired from the intelligence community and are living a quiet life in Spain. Maybe they're a junior aide in a political office, convinced their job is meaningless—until they see something they shouldn't. Or maybe they're right in the heart of the system already, working for a black ops unit or covering stories as a political journalist. Wherever they are, the first act is about creating tension between the life they *think* they're living and the life they're about to be dragged into.

Use ChatGPT to help you shape this opening moment. A simple prompt like, "Give me five ways a former intelligence agent could get pulled back into the field" can offer several interesting story starters. Maybe someone from their past resurfaces. Maybe they're named in a leaked file. Maybe someone leaves a burner phone on their doorstep that starts ringing at 2:00 a.m. It doesn't have to be big—it just has to be *wrong* enough to unsettle them.

Once that seed is planted, the first act is about resistance. Your protagonist shouldn't leap into the mission. They should resist it, question it, want to walk away from it. That tension—the push and pull—is what makes it feel real. They've been through this before. They know what it costs. They know that getting involved means giving up comfort, safety, and probably someone they care about. The mission, at this point, should feel like a curse, not a calling.

Also, this is your chance to show the reader the system your story is about to challenge. If it's a political thriller, reveal the world of politics—the speeches, the spin, the shadowy advisors, the smiling faces that hide agendas. If it's an espionage story, let us see the agency, the hierarchy, the secrecy. Let us feel the bureaucracy, the burned-out field agents, the surveillance culture. Let us smell the corruption in the air. Even if your protagonist isn't aware of the full scope yet, the reader should sense that something is off.

This is also the time to quietly plant clues. Not in a "wink at the audience" way, but in a way that will make sense later. The car that's been parked outside for too long. The name in a document that nobody explains. A slip of the tongue in a casual conversation. These details, when revealed to be important in the second or third act, give your story weight and cleverness. Ask ChatGPT to suggest subtle foreshadowing for your plot twist, and you'll get ideas for early-stage breadcrumbs that pay off later.

Now, in the best political and espionage thrillers, the mission doesn't come in the form of a dossier or an envelope with a red stamp. It comes as a *problem*. A mystery. A contradiction. Your hero sees something they can't explain—or worse, something they *can* explain but no one else is willing to acknowledge. The mission often starts with a single unanswered question. Why did that operative go dark? Why was that meeting off the books? Why is everyone pretending nothing is wrong?

The sooner you plant that question, the faster your plot takes off. And it should lead to another question. And then another. This is how the rabbit hole opens up. And before the protagonist knows it, they're in deeper than they ever expected to go. That's the essence of the genre: one simple discovery that leads to something monstrous. Something systemic. Something that someone very powerful is willing to kill to protect.

You can also use this act to build emotional stakes. Who does your protagonist care about? What would they be willing to give up to keep that person safe? What do they fear losing if the truth comes out? The sooner the reader understands what's personally at risk, the more powerful every plot twist becomes. The danger isn't just abstract—it's tied to someone the protagonist loves, or someone they lost, or something they believe in. Ask ChatGPT to generate a character with both a personal connection and a professional vulnerability. Maybe it's a sibling in the military. A spouse who works in the same agency. A child who asks too many questions. That emotional anchor will become the pulse of the story.

And by the end of the first act, your protagonist has to make a choice. Not to *solve* the mystery, but to stop running from it. To dig deeper. To meet someone in secret. To follow a lead. To go off the grid. This decision doesn't come easily. Maybe they're blackmailed into it. Maybe they're pulled in by guilt. Maybe someone close to them disappears. But the mission doesn't truly start until they stop looking away and take that first step toward the unknown.

That's where your story shifts from the known world to the clandestine one. The moment the ground falls out from under the protagonist—and the reader. The second act is about descent. But the first act? It's about setting the trap. Quietly, carefully, methodically. And then letting it spring.

In the next chapter, we'll explore how to write opening scenes that don't just inform—but hook. Because once you've set the groundwork, you only have one job: make it impossible for the reader to stop turning the page.

Crafting Your First Scene to Drop Readers in the Fire

Your first scene is your first strike. In a political or espionage thriller, you don't have the luxury of easing the reader in with a quiet day in the office or a slow coffee break. You've got to drop them right into a situation that smells like trouble. That doesn't mean explosions, gunfire, or rooftop chases—though it can—but more often, it means tension. A sense that something's off. Something's watching. Someone's lying. From the first sentence, the reader needs to feel like they've walked into a room mid-conversation, with secrets already in motion and danger waiting just outside the door.

This genre thrives on paranoia, ambiguity, and stakes that aren't immediately visible but definitely present. So your first scene is not just about opening a story—it's about plunging the reader into an atmosphere where they know the surface is a lie and the real story is hiding underneath. You want them to feel like they've picked up a file they weren't meant to see. Something classified. Something dangerous.

Let's talk strategy. Start with a moment of imbalance. Maybe someone is being watched but doesn't know it. Maybe a deal is being made with too many smiles. Maybe a coded message comes through in the middle of a party. This kind of moment plants a question without answering it. The reader doesn't need all the facts yet—they need to *feel* the tension. They need to sense the wire underfoot.

You can build a brilliant first scene even before you fully know the rest of your story. That's the beauty of using ChatGPT. You can tell it your premise, your protagonist, or even just your desired tone, and say, "Write an opening scene where my protagonist receives a message that disrupts their life." Or "Give me an atmospheric opening where nothing violent happens, but something's clearly wrong." You'll get a foundation to build on—something laced with unease that feels cinematic and sharp.

Let's say your thriller is about a foreign diplomat secretly feeding intel to a rogue faction. You don't open with a briefing about who they are. You open with them in an elevator, traveling upward with a briefcase, alone—until they realize the elevator is going somewhere it shouldn't. The silence. The flickering lights. The number panel skipping a floor. Their thumb brushing the phone in their pocket, not calling, just in case. You start in a moment that *feels* like the world is about to change.

Alternatively, maybe your story is more political. A journalist receives a routine press release—only it contains a name that shouldn't be there. Instead of reacting with shock, they freeze. They know what this means. They close the file, wipe their prints off the mouse, and walk out like nothing happened. The reader doesn't know the full implications, but they feel the shift. That's how you get them leaning in.

One powerful tool in your first scene is silence. Let things go unspoken. Show the reader something strange, but don't explain it. A character slipping a photo into their coat. A code phrase spoken during a toast. A file stamped "classified" with one corner burned. These elements don't shout—they whisper. And readers in this genre love whispers. They want to solve the puzzle. Your job is to give them just enough pieces to get hooked.

You can also use setting to establish tension. A government office after hours. A train station during a thunderstorm. A surveillance van parked on a street where it doesn't belong. The environment should reflect the mood—claustrophobic, uncertain, layered with meaning. Ask ChatGPT to describe a tense, atmospheric location for a political or espionage opening scene, and it'll give you suggestions that practically hum with potential.

Dialogue, too, can carry a lot of the early weight. But it shouldn't be about exposition. Think suggestion, misdirection, implication. Characters talking around something. A government official and an aide discussing a scheduled press conference while one of them slips a flash drive across the table with their thumb. A romantic partner asking a question that sounds casual but lands like a loaded gun. The subtext is what matters. Make the reader feel like they've stumbled into something halfway through—and now they're trying to catch up.

And don't forget—your first scene is also about tone. You're telling the reader what kind of experience they're about to have. If your thriller is high-energy espionage with globe-trotting action, maybe you do open mid-chase, a courier dodging bullets through the streets of Istanbul with a microchip tucked in his belt. If your story is more cerebral and political, maybe it starts with a private conversation in a limousine, where someone says one thing and clearly means another. Tone is your fingerprint. Get it right early, and the reader will follow you anywhere.

The first scene should leave the reader with more questions than answers, but it must also contain *one thing that matters*. A moment that sets the story in motion. It could be a call to action, a subtle betrayal, a small crack in the illusion. But something has to shift. Your hero doesn't need to understand what's happening—not yet—but the ground beneath them should tremble just enough to warn them that they've stepped into something far bigger than they realized.

Use ChatGPT to help you refine that final beat. Ask: "Give me five ways this opening scene could end with tension rising, even if nothing explodes." That kind of prompt can help you craft a last moment that stays with the reader. A look exchanged. A door left ajar. A sentence that hangs just a little too long in the air.

By the time your reader hits the second chapter, they should be hooked. Not because they know everything, but because they know *something*—and they want more. That's what your first scene is for. To pull them into the fire without them even realizing how close they are to the burn.

Next, we'll dive into how to build the world your story lives in—the locations, institutions, and systems of control that give your thriller its authenticity and edge. Because in this genre, setting isn't just background. It's leverage. It's surveillance. It's a character in its own right.

The World of Secrets: Choosing the Right Setting

In political and espionage thrillers, the setting is never just wallpaper. It's a weapon. It's a trap. It's a vault for information and a maze for misdirection. The right setting doesn't just hold the story—it amplifies it. It reflects the tone, complicates the action, and adds a layer of meaning to every conversation, every betrayal, every silent decision. In this genre, the world you choose isn't passive—it's alive, observing, recording, waiting to betray or protect your characters. Which means you can't afford to treat it like a throwaway detail.

The first thing to know about choosing the right setting is this: your story's tension lives where power and secrecy overlap. Wherever control is enforced and truth is hidden, you have a potential goldmine for political and spy fiction. These stories thrive in boardrooms, intelligence bunkers, embassies, airports, crowded streets, diplomatic summits, abandoned factories, safehouses, and stately homes with backdoor deals. Think of every location as a piece of the story's operating system. It's not just about where the action happens—it's about how the space controls or confines the people inside it.

One way to approach setting selection is to divide your world into *three zones*: the public, the private, and the classified. The public is where people pretend. These are the places your characters wear masks—press conferences, award galas, city squares, places of performative transparency. The private is where deals are whispered and truths begin to slip out—high-security offices, hotel rooms, private jets, surveillance vans. The classified is where the gloves come off: underground facilities, war rooms, detention sites, secret labs, remote compounds. Every zone changes how your characters act, and every one can be a crucible for tension if you choose carefully.

Let's say your story is a political thriller centered around a conspiracy within the highest levels of government. You could choose Washington D.C., but you'd want to go deeper than the White House or Capitol Hill. Ask ChatGPT to generate less obvious but highly symbolic locations—perhaps a high-level think tank in Georgetown, a restaurant known for political meetups, or the archive room of a private security firm. These kinds of settings give your story texture and believability. They feel researched, even when they're invented.

If you're leaning into espionage, the world gets even more interesting. Spies move through cities like smoke—London, Berlin, Istanbul, Hong Kong, Moscow. Why? Because these places are crossroads. Historical, political, and economic tension converge there. But even within those cities, there's room for specificity. A crumbling Cold War-era safe house. A metro tunnel converted into a data hub. A rooftop where two agents meet beneath neon lights and rain. Ask ChatGPT to describe "five espionage settings in Berlin that could be used for a secret exchange," and suddenly your scene writes itself.

You should also think about how your setting *controls behavior*. A political summit in a luxurious European hotel? Everyone's on edge. Everyone's being watched. One wrong handshake can cause an international incident. A border crossing in a war-torn country? Tension's baked in. The environment isn't just background—it dictates the rhythm of dialogue, the flow of movement, the rules of engagement. In a story like this, geography *is* psychology. Use it to your advantage.

And don't underestimate contrast. Sometimes, the most chilling scenes happen in the quietest places. A coded message passed during a school recital. A murder staged to look like an accident at a garden party. The use of familiar, even comforting settings to deliver shocking plot points is a hallmark of the genre. It lulls the audience into a false sense of safety before pulling the rug out from under them. ChatGPT can help brainstorm these ironic environments with prompts like, "Give me peaceful locations where high-stakes espionage scenes could unfold unexpectedly."

Technology also plays a role in your setting. A modern thriller might use a surveillance drone, a phone tapped in real-time, a video conference hacked by a third party. These things need believable spaces to operate in. Think about data centers hidden beneath corporations, embassies with soundproof meeting rooms, smart homes designed to spy on their owners. The setting should reflect the paranoia and digital control we now live with—especially in political thrillers, where data is power.

Cultural and political layers can add even more tension. Maybe your story is set in a country teetering on the edge of collapse. Maybe your spy operates in a region where language barriers, religious customs, or historic grudges shape every interaction. The world of secrets isn't only about the buildings—it's about the systems that run underneath them. Ask ChatGPT to generate locations based on current geopolitical tensions or to describe the atmosphere of a fictional authoritarian city. You'll get environments that drip with pressure before the first scene even unfolds.

Symbolism matters, too. Maybe your final act takes place in the ruins of a palace that once represented peace. Maybe the betrayal happens in a cathedral, a stark clash between the sacred and the profane. Maybe a deal is made in an old courtroom that once housed war crimes trials. When your settings are emotionally or politically charged, they do double duty—creating atmosphere and reinforcing theme.

And don't forget the value of *movement*. The thriller genre loves to move: trains, planes, convoys, motorcades, boats in fog, cars at midnight. Mobile settings create their own challenges and energy. Characters are forced into confined quarters. Clocks start ticking. Plans change in real time. Ask ChatGPT to help plan a story that unfolds across multiple countries or along a travel route, and you'll find that geography becomes part of the plot architecture itself.

In this genre, the world isn't just a place your story happens. It's a character. It hides things. It lies. It pressures. It exposes. Whether you choose sterile government halls or dim alleys in a border town, the setting should always carry tension, meaning, and the ever-present sense that someone—or something—is watching.

In the next chapter, we'll talk about building a believable political system or intelligence structure to support your story—because once your setting is chosen, you need to populate it with institutions, hierarchies, and shadows that move the story forward with deadly precision.

Spy Agencies, Dictatorships, and Rogue Governments

In a political or espionage thriller, the danger isn't always a man with a gun. Sometimes it's a government that listens to your every call, watches your every move, and rewrites truth with the stroke of a pen. Sometimes it's an intelligence agency that doesn't answer to laws. Sometimes it's a regime that claims to protect its people but operates like a machine of silence, suppression, and surveillance. These forces—real or fictional—aren't just backdrops. They are the antagonistic systems that your protagonist must navigate, outsmart, and sometimes survive. When written well, they don't feel like fiction. They feel like warnings.

Let's start with spy agencies—the lifeblood of the espionage thriller. Whether you're writing about a real-world agency like the CIA, MI6, Mossad, or FSB, or a fictional intelligence group that operates in the shadows, the key is believability. These agencies aren't just collections of agents. They're bureaucracies with rival departments, internal agendas, and political pressure constantly shaping what they do—and more importantly, what they *don't* do. The best thrillers understand that spy agencies aren't monoliths. There's conflict within them. One division might be going rogue. Another might be trying to shut down the very operation your hero is caught up in.

Use ChatGPT to sketch out the internal structure of a fictional agency. You can ask for roles, divisions, and the kinds of operations they oversee. Give it a name that sounds clinical and forgettable—those always hide the dirtiest secrets. Think: Directorate of External Liaison. Or Bureau 7. Or simply "Section." Then decide what makes this agency dangerous. Do they have no oversight? Do they answer directly to one person? Are they privately funded? Are they slowly becoming militarized? These traits matter. They shape how far the agency will go—and how alone your protagonist will be if they cross it.

Now let's bring in the governments that give these agencies their teeth. In political thrillers, you often deal with regimes that operate behind smiling press conferences. They hold elections, but the outcomes are rigged. They shake hands with allies while assassinating dissidents in back alleys. These can be based on real countries or fictional composites, but the more detailed they are, the more threatening they feel. Ask ChatGPT to build a fictional authoritarian regime: its ruling party, propaganda strategy, internal surveillance systems, and the mythology it feeds its citizens. The more complete the illusion, the more devastating it is when your protagonist begins to see the cracks.

Dictatorships add a different kind of threat to your story. They make every conversation risky. Every room potentially bugged. Every ally a possible spy. They don't need to send armies after your hero—they can ruin them with one whispered rumor or a forced confession aired on national TV. These regimes often have a public image they carefully maintain, which creates great opportunities for dramatic irony. The leader praised for "peace through strength" might be the same one ordering covert assassinations abroad. The minister of culture might secretly fund propaganda, rewriting history in real time.

Then there's the wildcard of rogue governments. These are states that operate outside international norms—sometimes recognized by the world, sometimes ignored. Maybe they're developing weapons in secret. Maybe they've been quietly funding cyberattacks. Maybe they're trying to influence foreign elections through shell companies and dark money. Rogue states aren't defined by location—they're defined by *motive*. They believe the rules don't apply to them, and that belief makes them incredibly volatile.

You can also write about rogue factions *within* legitimate governments. Maybe it's a breakaway military division, a faction of radical politicians, or a black budget project so deeply buried that not even the president knows it exists. These groups operate with partial access to state power, but without accountability. They have funding, personnel, equipment—but no leash. And when your hero starts pulling on the wrong thread, these are the people who come knocking in the night.

One powerful strategy is to blur the lines between good and evil institutions. Maybe your protagonist works for an agency that claims to defend freedom—but begins to realize they're part of something darker. Or maybe the so-called enemy nation turns out to be more honest about its intentions than your protagonist's own government. This moral uncertainty is what elevates the genre. It forces your characters—and your readers—to ask, "What's the real difference between us and them?"

Don't forget how these systems shape characters. A field agent from a corrupt agency might start to crack under guilt. A journalist operating in a dictatorship might speak carefully in every conversation, always wondering who's listening. A politician trying to expose the truth might find themselves surveilled, smeared, or suddenly silenced by bureaucratic machinery. The characters aren't just shaped by the plot—they're shaped by the institutions breathing down their necks.

And here's where ChatGPT becomes a force multiplier. Ask it to generate government structures, rival spy networks, secret treaties, or even cold war-era sleeper cells that were never deactivated. Ask it to create fictional countries with real-world parallels. You'll get a landscape of corruption and control that feels eerily familiar, even when it's fictional. That's the key—your world of secrets should feel *possible*, even when it's imaginary.

The presence of these powerful systems raises the stakes of every scene. When a character speaks out, they're not just risking a gun to the head—they're risking blackmail, exile, the erasure of their identity. When they run, they don't just run from men—they run from entire networks of surveillance, influence, and legal impunity. And when they fight, they don't just fight one person—they fight a machine that's been devouring people like them for years.

Building a Political System that Fuels the Conflict

A great political or espionage thriller doesn't just rely on characters and action—it runs on the slow-burning fuel of the system itself. The deeper the system, the bigger the stakes. Whether you're writing about a corrupt democracy, a crumbling dictatorship, or a government on the brink of civil collapse, your political structure should do more than sit in the background. It should *generate* the story. It should make characters paranoid, drive people to betrayal, and force your protagonist into impossible choices. When the political system is a living, breathing part of the narrative, your thriller becomes more than just a race—it becomes a statement.

Start by defining the bones of your system. Is this a democracy, an oligarchy, a monarchy disguised as a republic? Does it look free on paper but operate under layers of unseen control? Or is it open about its authoritarianism—proud of the order it maintains by watching every citizen? Whatever model you choose, don't just copy the real world. Build *your* version of it. Even if it's based on reality, let it have its own flavor. You're not writing a documentary. You're writing a world where truth is currency and power is poison.

Use ChatGPT to sketch the architecture of your fictional government. Ask it to design a five-tier bureaucracy for a "post-democratic surveillance state," or outline the structure of a coalition government riddled with secret deals. You'll get departments, figureheads, shadow organizations, even fake ministries—all of which can be used to create tension and conspiracy. The goal isn't complexity for its own sake—it's to create a web that your protagonist has to navigate, climb, or cut through.

Every good system has *pressure points*. These are the cracks in the walls—the places where corruption thrives, where whistle-blowers hide, where secrets can leak. Maybe the justice department is politically compromised. Maybe the intelligence community answers to no one. Maybe elections are manipulated through corporate influence or foreign interference. These weak spots aren't just window dressing. They're *entry points* for your plot. That's where your hero begins pulling the thread—and where everything starts to unravel.

One powerful trick is to decide who the public face of power is... and who's really in charge. Maybe the prime minister is a puppet for the intelligence chief. Maybe the president is compromised by foreign debt. Maybe a corporate lobbyist, a media mogul, or a military contractor has more control over policy than any elected official. Letting your protagonist slowly realize who's really pulling the strings gives your story a constantly evolving threat.

Then there's *ideology*. What does this system believe? Or, more importantly, what does it *pretend* to believe? A political system needs a myth to survive. A story it tells the people to justify its power. Maybe it preaches unity while secretly dividing citizens by class, race, or loyalty. Maybe it claims to protect the constitution while systematically rewriting it in secret. Maybe it worships security above all, turning surveillance into patriotism. These myths become part of the setting, the dialogue, the propaganda posters, and the fake news headlines.

Ask ChatGPT to help craft the public narrative versus the private reality. A prompt like, "Create a fictional government that claims to be a protector of freedom but suppresses dissidents," can give you both the slogans and the dirty truth beneath them. These contradictions are your story's tension points. When your hero starts to see behind the curtain, they don't just fight a person—they fight a belief system.

Don't forget the mechanics of how this system *protects itself*. Governments in this genre are paranoid by design. They have counterintelligence departments, disinformation units, legal instruments that can ruin lives with a signature. You can use ChatGPT to generate tactics used by fictional regimes to maintain control—controlled media narratives, fake terrorist threats, manipulated elections, secret courts, or even digital blackmail databases. These aren't just flavor—they're weapons your protagonist might face, or tools your villain might use.

A solid political system also provides endless character types. You've got loyal bureaucrats who believe in the mission, idealists trying to reform from the inside, burnt-out advisors who've seen too much, and turncoats who profit from playing both sides. These people are shaped by the system—and, in turn, shape it. They're not just side characters. They're part of the machinery your protagonist is up against. Give them real motivations. Maybe they don't think they're evil. Maybe they think they're saving the country. That complexity makes every conversation crackle with meaning.

And then, of course, there's the public. The people the system is supposed to serve—or manipulate. Are they complicit? Apathetic? Enraged but powerless? Are there protests on the street, or does everyone pretend not to see what's going on? Maybe the population is divided—some who fear change, others who demand revolution. You can ask ChatGPT to describe how different classes or regions react to your fictional political system. This adds texture, realism, and fuel for subplots.

Finally, your system should create moral pressure. Your protagonist isn't just dodging bullets—they're confronting their own values. Maybe they used to believe in the system. Maybe they helped build it. Maybe they want to change it, but the closer they get to the truth, the more they realize how deep the rot goes. This is the moment where your hero has to decide: expose the truth and burn everything down... or become part of the lie to survive.

The best political systems in thrillers aren't just corrupt—they're *designed* to make resistance feel pointless. But that's what makes it so satisfying when your hero decides to fight anyway. Even if they lose, the fight matters. The truth matters. The system *must* be challenged. That's where the heart of the genre lives.

In the next chapter, we'll dive into the physical and mental conditioning that your hero might have gone through—because to navigate this world of lies and shadows, your protagonist needs more than willpower. They need training that was never meant to be used in the light.

Training Your Operative: Martial Arts, Guns, and Mind Games

In the world of espionage and political thrillers, your protagonist isn't just someone who stumbles into danger—they're someone forged in it. Whether they're an ex-operative, an active agent, or a civilian who's been trained for a very specific kind of war, they've been taught to survive, manipulate, and fight in ways the average person can't even imagine. And while your story isn't a manual, it *feels* more authentic when your operative doesn't just shoot straight and throw punches—they think tactically, they adapt instinctively, and they've been trained to be invisible in plain sight.

Let's break it down: your operative's training is what makes them both compelling and dangerous. It's not just about action—it's about control. A trained operative knows when not to pull the trigger. They know how to use violence as a last resort, not a first reaction. They are designed to assess, manipulate, and neutralize threats, both physically and psychologically. That training adds tension to every scene, because it creates the possibility that they're ten steps ahead—even when they're seemingly powerless.

First, let's talk combat. A believable operative isn't a martial arts master with flashy spin-kicks and wire-fu. They're fast, efficient, and brutal. Their hand-to-hand skills are built on close-combat disciplines like Krav Maga, Systema, or military combatives. These styles prioritize disarming, disabling, and neutralizing with the least amount of motion. If your character gets into a fight, it's not about choreography—it's about survival. An elbow to the throat. A joint lock to control a weapon. A knee to the groin followed by a chokehold. That's the language of real-world fight training.

You can use ChatGPT to help describe a specific fighting style. Ask for a breakdown of "how a former Navy SEAL would neutralize an attacker in a tight space," and you'll get move-by-move logic that can anchor your scene. These details—when kept quick, sharp, and grounded—elevate the authenticity of your story without turning it into a combat manual.

Next, guns. Your protagonist knows how to handle firearms, but they're not doing dramatic reloads or spraying bullets. They fire only when they have to, and they aim to end the threat instantly. Pistols for close work, carbines for longer engagements, and maybe a suppressed weapon for stealth. But the real value in gun training comes from tactical awareness. Knowing how to clear a room, scan for threats, maintain cover, and account for crossfire. It's about logic and discipline, not Hollywood chaos.

Ask ChatGPT for real-world tactical movements or weapons loadouts based on your character's background. A former intelligence agent might favor concealed carry, small-caliber weapons, or easily disposable tools. A military-trained operative might think in terms of fields of fire, fallback plans, and exfiltration points. Give your character a relationship with their weapon. Do they name it? Do they hate it? Do they carry it with reverence or as a reminder of something they lost?

But beyond the physical, the most important aspect of your operative's training is *mental*. Espionage is a psychological game, and your character has been trained to lie, read microexpressions, handle interrogation, resist manipulation, and play multiple personas. This is where the spy really becomes dangerous—not because they can shoot, but because they can *control* a room with silence. They can pretend to be weak when they're watching everything. They can get someone to trust them in five minutes, then disappear forever.

Interrogation training, emotional control, and even psychological conditioning become tools your protagonist carries at all times. Maybe they've been trained to control their heartrate, or to dissociate under stress. Maybe they've practiced acting out fake emotional reactions—panic, grief, rage—so well that even a trained observer wouldn't know the difference. Maybe they've been taught to pass polygraph tests, or flip between accents and mannerisms like masks. That kind of training creates endless possibilities for deception, infiltration, and internal conflict.

Use ChatGPT to simulate training regimens. A prompt like, "Describe the psychological conditioning of a spy trained to resist torture and manipulation" can give you insights that shape how your protagonist reacts under pressure. These aren't just facts—they're story fuel. When your hero is captured, you now know how they behave. When they interrogate someone else, you know what games they're playing. When they're in a crowd, you know what they're scanning for.

There's also the moral side of training. Real operatives are often taught to detach from the outcome. To complete the mission. To suppress empathy. That's where the cracks begin to show. Maybe your protagonist is trained to see everyone as a potential asset or threat, but starts to fall for someone. Maybe they've been conditioned to kill without hesitation—but now they hesitate. That tension between training and humanity is where the character becomes not just interesting, but *human.*

Training can also isolate. When your character is surrounded by civilians or even other agents, there's a sense that they can never truly be themselves. They're always scanning, always measuring risk. That kind of constant control is exhausting. Let your character have moments where they try to feel normal—and fail. Let them flinch at sudden noises. Let them forget how to talk casually. Let them go blank when someone touches them unexpectedly. These behaviors show the *cost* of training, not just the utility.

And of course, training can be used against them. Maybe the antagonist is someone who *knows* their training—because they went through it too. Maybe their tactics are predictable because they were taught to act a certain way. That kind of mirrored dynamic creates great tension. Two trained operatives facing each other across a table, bluffing, waiting, watching for the tell that gives the other away.

In the end, your protagonist's training should feel like both an asset and a burden. It helps them survive—but it also keeps them from connecting, from healing, from letting go. They don't walk into danger—they *are* the danger. But they're also the one person who knows just how much danger the world is really in. That kind of character doesn't need a big entrance. They just need a quiet moment, a hard stare, and a sense that if they really wanted to, they could end the conversation—and maybe the person—right there.

In the next chapter, we'll explore how to give your operative a signature combat style or technique that defines them in action. Because in a genre built on shadows and subtlety, nothing speaks louder than the way someone chooses to fight.

Creating a Signature Combat Style for Your Spy

When you're writing an espionage or political thriller, your protagonist's combat style says more about them than any dossier. It's not just about how they fight—it's about who they are, what they've survived, what they fear, and what kind of training molded them into a weapon. A signature combat style becomes part of the character's identity. It makes action scenes feel tailored, personal, and full of subtext. It separates your hero from the crowd of generic action operatives by giving them a unique rhythm, method, or tactical preference that reflects both personality and purpose.

Not every spy needs to be flashy. In fact, the best ones rarely are. They don't fight to impress. They fight to win—and to disappear. Their combat style is a reflection of efficiency, resourcefulness, and control. And the more layered and consistent it is, the more believable and gripping your story becomes.

Start by considering their *background*. A former military operative might be built around brute force and battlefield tactics. Someone trained by an intelligence agency could be more surgical—striking fast, escaping faster. A character who grew up in the streets might fight dirty, using improvised weapons, striking where it hurts the most. Their past influences their instincts. Ask yourself: who taught them how to fight, and what kind of enemies did they train to face?

Use ChatGPT to create a unique fighting profile. Try a prompt like, "Give me a close-combat fighting style for a spy trained by a secretive Cold War-era program designed for silent assassinations." The AI can return not only the techniques but also the philosophy—whether the operative avoids confrontation altogether, prefers to disable rather than kill, or uses violence only as a psychological tool. These insights can shape how your character moves through the world.

Then think about *weapons of choice*. Some spies are experts with blades—silent, quick, precise. Others rely on handguns with suppressors, or favor non-lethal takedowns. A few use anything within reach—a rolled-up magazine, a belt, a wine bottle. Maybe your character always carries a collapsible baton in their jacket, or a garrote wire sewn into their sleeve. Maybe they don't carry weapons at all, because they *are* the weapon. Choosing a signature tool tells the reader a lot. A character who carries a combat knife is expecting to get up close and personal. One who carries cyanide capsules may not expect to survive the mission.

Style isn't just about tools, though—it's about *tempo*. Is your spy lightning-fast, favoring explosive motion followed by total stillness? Are they patient and predator-like, stalking from shadows, striking when the odds tip in their favor? Or are they a brawler, someone who's been in so many ugly fights that grace gave way to grit? You can describe action scenes with this rhythm in mind. Readers may not know the name of every move, but they'll *feel* the tone. A quick succession of short, sharp sentences can mimic a brutal close-quarters fight. Long, tense lines with observational detail suggest a methodical approach.

Another defining factor: *philosophy*. What is your spy's relationship with violence? Are they clinical and detached? Do they shut down emotionally while fighting? Do they secretly *enjoy* the fight, because it's the one place where everything makes sense? Do they avoid eye contact with the people they hurt, or do they look directly at them? This emotional layer makes their combat style more than just a collection of moves—it turns it into a window into their soul.

Sometimes it's the restraint that defines a signature style. Maybe your spy always disables instead of killing. Maybe they only shoot when the gun is pressed against the target's chest. Maybe they use silence as a weapon—taking out enemies so quietly that no one knows until it's too late. Maybe they have a rule: no killing unless absolutely necessary. And maybe, at some point in your story, they *have* to break that rule—and everything changes. That's the power of a signature approach. It creates a *code*, and codes are meant to be tested.

Signature styles can also emerge from *disabilities or limitations*. Maybe your character has an old injury, so they favor one side of their body, or avoid grappling. Maybe they suffer from PTSD, and only become violent under pressure, fighting in bursts that are unpredictable and overwhelming. These traits don't weaken the spy—they make them more real. Readers remember the flaws and the workarounds. They remember how the character *adapted*.

Environment plays a part, too. Maybe your character fights best in confined spaces—bathrooms, elevators, tight corridors. Maybe they need chaos—city streets, crowded markets—to mask their movements. Or maybe they use water, shadows, or elevation as part of their method. Ask ChatGPT to describe environments where a particular combat style would thrive, and then drop your character into that terrain. Let the world play to their strengths—or throw them into places that strip those strengths away.

There's also *signature moves*—little habits or behaviors that return across the story. Maybe your spy always goes for the throat first. Maybe they punch once, never twice, and then move to the next threat. Maybe they flip a ring on their finger before engaging, like a mental trigger. These small gestures become shorthand for the audience. When they appear, the reader knows something's about to happen—and it builds tension before the first punch is thrown.

Use ChatGPT to brainstorm three-to-five unique tactics or habits your spy uses in a fight. You might get ideas like a character who blinds enemies with pocketed sand before engaging, or one who always ends a fight with a pressure-point knockout. The point isn't to be flashy—it's to be *memorable*.

At the end of the day, a signature combat style is about turning violence into character. It's not what your spy does—it's *how* they do it, and *why*. That's what readers remember. Not just that the spy fought their way out of a building, but that they did it silently, methodically, never making eye contact, and left without a scratch. Or that they took a beating just to get close enough to whisper something in the enemy's ear before breaking their neck.

The fight tells us who the character really is when the mask drops.

Equipping Your Spy with Tools, Gadgets, and Tech

In espionage and political thrillers, your protagonist doesn't just survive on instinct—they survive on gear. Tools, gadgets, and cutting-edge tech aren't just props in these stories; they're extensions of the character's training, intelligence, and adaptability. The right piece of equipment, used at the right time, can change the course of a mission, save a life, or blow a conspiracy wide open. But the key to writing spy gear well is subtlety. Less James Bond fantasy, more modern-day plausibility with a shadowy edge.

A well-equipped spy doesn't carry a utility belt of sci-fi nonsense. They carry the essentials—items chosen for silence, utility, concealment, and deniability. Their gear is compact, multifunctional, and often disposable. It's gear designed to vanish when they do. Each tool your spy carries should tell you something about their background, their operating style, and their mindset.

Let's start with **the basics**. Most field operatives carry what's called a "go kit" or "gray man loadout." This includes everyday objects with hidden functions: a smartphone that doubles as a signal jammer, a keychain that can pick locks, a pen that hides a fiber-optic camera, or a wallet that conceals a razor-thin blade. These aren't flashy—they're smart. The kind of items that pass through airport security unnoticed and can get someone out of a jam when things go sideways.

ChatGPT can be incredibly useful for brainstorming these kinds of items. Try a prompt like, "List ten plausible real-world spy gadgets that can be concealed in everyday items," and you'll get a blend of creative and functional gear, all grounded in reality. From a lipstick with a hidden GPS tracker to a cigarette lighter that acts as a voice recorder, the options are endless—and all it takes is a few clever touches to make your character feel like they're living on the edge of modern surveillance warfare.

Then there's **surveillance and counter-surveillance tech**. If your story involves tailing someone or tracking assets, equip your spy with tools like a monocular-range laser microphone to pick up conversations through windows, a disguised drone for aerial reconnaissance, or an AI-based face-blurring app to slip through CCTV. On the flip side, give them tools to detect surveillance: radio frequency scanners, thermal imagers to spot hidden cameras, or a wristwatch that vibrates when GPS tracking is detected.

Another great angle is **communication gear**. In a world where digital signals are traceable, your spy needs tools for secure, deniable conversations. Think disposable encrypted phones, offline messaging tools like mesh network radios, or covert communication systems like Morse-code tapping through a coffee cup. Maybe your character has access to tech that scrambles video feeds, or to quantum-encrypted earpieces that relay real-time intelligence. These kinds of gadgets don't just add flair—they increase tension, especially when they *fail* at a critical moment.

Of course, **weapons technology** will be part of the loadout—but again, think quiet, concealable, and practical. A small-caliber handgun with a threaded barrel for a suppressor. A ceramic knife that doesn't show up on metal detectors. A one-shot pen gun used in tight quarters. Or maybe your operative uses chemical weapons—like aerosolized knockout agents hidden in perfume bottles. You don't need a dozen weapons. Just a few—unique, signature, and deadly.

And don't forget **tracking and tagging equipment**. Think GPS chips embedded in shoe soles, RFID tags sewn into clothing, or tracker darts fired from a compact launcher disguised as a car key. Maybe your protagonist uses tiny magnetic microphones that can be flicked onto vehicles as they pass. These tools create fantastic opportunities for scenes that rely on quiet pursuit or remote observation, and they also bring in the creeping paranoia that defines the genre.

Then we get to **digital infiltration tools**. Hacking is no longer a side skill—it's part of modern tradecraft. Your spy might carry a USB rubber ducky that injects malicious code into any computer, a fake charger that downloads data from nearby phones, or a keylogger disguised as a charging cable. Or maybe they use Bluetooth-based spoofing tools to hijack phone calls or copy data from air-gapped devices. This kind of tech lets your story pivot into cyber espionage territory without losing the gritty realism.

ChatGPT is excellent at helping build fictional versions of these tools. You can ask it, "Invent a plausible new spy gadget that would be used in a modern political thriller," and get something that toes the line between speculative and believable. Maybe you invent a biometric-cloning patch that mimics someone's fingerprint for thirty seconds. Or a fabric that masks a person's heat signature from infrared detection. These tools, if used sparingly, add a speculative edge without pushing the story into science fiction.

Don't underestimate **low-tech tools**, either. Paper maps with invisible ink. A fake business card that unlocks a safe. A Zippo lighter with a hidden USB stick. These items carry charm, and they reinforce the idea that your character is adaptable. They don't rely on one kind of tech—they mix old-school tradecraft with modern tools. That duality is what makes a great spy feel grounded. They're not just someone with gadgets—they're someone who knows how to use whatever's available.

And finally, **failure** is what makes gear interesting. Don't make everything work perfectly. Let the comms unit lose signal in a tunnel. Let the suppressor jam. Let the facial recognition spoof glitch mid-infiltration. That's what adds suspense. It's not just about what gear your spy carries—it's about how they respond when it fails, and they're left with nothing but their wits and whatever they can scavenge.

Your operative's toolkit should feel like a story in itself. Each item tells us who they are, where they've been, and what they expect to face. Are they over-prepared or minimalist? Do they rely on tech, or do they trust their instincts more? Are they still using gear from their old agency, even though they're off the grid? Or have they gone fully rogue, building their own gadgets from scratch?

In the next chapter, we'll pivot from the gear to the enemy's territory—discussing how to write infiltration scenes that use your spy's tools, skills, and wit to get past layers of security, both digital and human. Because getting inside is one thing. Getting out alive is another.

Breaking and Entering: Planning Infiltration Scenes

Infiltration scenes are the heartbeat of any great espionage or political thriller. They're where silence becomes suspense, where the ticking of a watch or the creak of a floorboard can be more intense than gunfire. Done right, a break-in isn't just a plot beat—it's a symphony of tension, skill, precision, and risk. And it's where your protagonist truly earns their stripes. Whether they're slipping into a foreign embassy, a heavily guarded tech lab, or a corrupt official's penthouse, the infiltration scene is where your story tightens like a noose.

The first step in writing these scenes is understanding that **infiltration is not improvisation**—at least not entirely. A good operative studies the target, plans every step, runs contingency options, and even memorizes the habits of the guards or the cleaning crew. There's an intelligence-gathering phase that leads up to the moment the character steps over the threshold. Use ChatGPT to simulate this process. Ask it, "How would a trained spy break into a high-security office without being detected?" and build that prep into the story before the action begins.

When designing the infiltration, start by asking three key questions:

What is the objective?

What are the obstacles?

What are the consequences of failure?

Your operative might be after data, a physical object, a person, or even just a photograph. Whatever it is, make it specific, make it urgent, and make it hard to reach. Then layer the defenses—security guards, motion sensors, biometric scanners, cameras, dogs, environmental factors like darkness or weather. The more layered the security, the more satisfying it is to watch your protagonist peel through it one layer at a time.

Your character's approach will tell us a lot about who they are. Do they avoid every encounter, ghosting through hallways unseen? Or do they quietly take down guards one by one? Are they methodical, rehearsed, and clinical—or reckless, improvisational, and desperate? Ask ChatGPT for personality-based tactics: "Describe how an emotionally detached spy would infiltrate a military compound," or "Show how a rogue agent with PTSD might break into a secure lab." You'll get insight that turns the sequence into character development, not just plot progression.

Timing is everything. Maybe your spy enters during a shift change, when security is momentarily distracted. Maybe they move during a blackout, a thunderstorm, or a political protest happening outside. Infiltration often relies on exploiting moments of chaos, however minor. And the tension builds best when the protagonist is operating on a deadline—when the guard will return in 90 seconds, when the lights will flicker back on in two minutes, when the extraction team is circling overhead and won't wait long.

The **environment** should feel like a character in itself. A dark museum filled with pressure sensors. A concrete government building with voice-activated locks. A derelict hotel repurposed into a surveillance hub. Make the space tactile and immersive. Let your protagonist navigate the smells, the sounds, the lighting. Let them count their footsteps. Let them notice the sound of their own breathing. The more grounded the setting, the more the reader leans forward in their seat.

Use **tech wisely but sparingly**. Yes, your operative might use a thermal scanner, a remote hack, or a jammer—but tech should *assist* the infiltration, not solve it. Let the reader feel the pressure when the fingerprint spoof takes too long to process or the drone battery starts to die. Let gear fail at the worst possible moment. That's how you make readers hold their breath.

And don't forget **human threats**. A sleepy guard. A curious janitor. A security analyst watching monitors but distracted by a phone call. These are opportunities for tension and subversion. Maybe your character has to lie on the spot. Maybe they pretend to be someone they're not. Maybe they have to knock someone out and hide the body in an office closet. Every human interaction is a potential complication—and a chance to show off your spy's nerves, improvisation, or restraint.

Use ChatGPT to create complications. Ask, "What are five unpredictable obstacles a spy might face during a break-in at a government facility?" You'll get everything from unexpected visitors to power outages to the sudden arrival of someone your operative knows personally. Those twists are what take a break-in from good to unforgettable.

Infiltration scenes also benefit from **tight pacing**. You don't need long blocks of exposition here. You need sensory detail, internal monologue, and the occasional ticking clock. Sentences should feel like steps. Paragraphs should mimic breath control. The pacing becomes part of the suspense. The reader should feel like they're inside the mission, heartbeat matching the tension on the page.

And then, of course, there's the **escape**. It's one thing to get in. It's another to get out. Sometimes the exit is clean—your protagonist disappears into the night with what they came for. But more often, this is where things go wrong. A locked door. An alarm that didn't trigger on the way in but does on the way out. Reinforcements arriving. The discovery of something far worse than they were expecting. Let the exit strategy fall apart just enough to raise the stakes.

If you want to push it further, twist the entire mission. What if they were never meant to succeed? What if someone *let* them in? What if the item they're stealing is bait? The break-in becomes not the climax, but the catalyst for a deeper conspiracy. These reversals keep readers guessing and transform a tense scene into a turning point.

Infiltration isn't just about sneaking in—it's about tension, control, risk, and the constant threat of exposure. It's where your spy becomes more than just a character with a gun or a plan. It's where they show what they're really made of.

In the next chapter, we'll shift gears into the escape and evasion stage—because once the alarm sounds and the net starts tightening, the only thing that matters is staying ahead of the hunt. That's where instinct, planning, and raw adrenaline collide.

Escape and Evasion: Writing Tactical Retreats

Every good spy knows the truth: getting in is only half the job. It's getting out that makes or breaks a mission. Escape and evasion isn't about retreat—it's about survival under pressure, disappearing under fire, and turning a failed mission into a living memory. In political and espionage thrillers, these moments are where the story's pace spikes, the stakes explode, and the mask of control slips—if only for a moment. This isn't running away. This is fighting to stay in the game.

Writing an effective escape scene begins with one essential ingredient: **everything just went wrong**. Maybe the guard who was supposed to be asleep is awake. Maybe the extraction window closed early. Maybe the data they were sent to steal was a trap, or the person they were supposed to save is already dead. Whatever the trigger, the key to this chapter is escalation. Let the floor collapse beneath your protagonist. They trained for the perfect entry, but now they're improvising under fire. That's when the adrenaline kicks in—for them and the reader.

Start with the **environment**. Where are they escaping from? A cramped office building at night, a mountain compound in the snow, an embassy crawling with surveillance? Each setting dictates a different kind of retreat. In a city, they might lose themselves in a crowd, duck into alleyways, or jump between rooftops. In a remote location, they might have to evade search parties, survive off the land, or radio for emergency extraction. Use ChatGPT to model escape strategies for specific environments. Try a prompt like, "How would a spy escape from a surveillance-heavy embassy in downtown Berlin?" and build your scene around the suggested tactics.

Next, let's talk **rhythm**. Escape scenes shouldn't be one long sprint—they're about movement, but also about pauses, decisions, redirections. Maybe your character runs down one path, only to double back. Maybe they switch clothes, change posture, blend in. Maybe they freeze and let the danger pass inches away. These scenes need to breathe, just like your character does. Quick action followed by stillness. Loud chaos followed by deafening quiet. That contrast creates the tension you want.

Then there's **what they leave behind**. A good escape is always about sacrifice. Maybe they have to drop the intel. Maybe they're forced to leave a teammate behind. Maybe they fake their own death, burning a cover they've had for years. Every tactical retreat has a cost, and that cost adds emotional weight. Use it to grow the character, not just push the plot forward.

Think in terms of **tactical improvisation**. Your character didn't plan for this. So what do they do when the plan breaks? Maybe they pull a fire alarm to trigger chaos. Maybe they set a timed distraction—blowing a transformer, cutting the lights, or triggering a false signal. Maybe they bribe someone with cash or secrets. You can ask ChatGPT to give you "creative distraction techniques for escaping a secure facility," and you'll be surprised at how many layered, plausible options you'll get.

And of course, the **chase**. Not every evasion needs to turn into a chase scene—but when it does, make it visceral. Let the reader feel the footfalls, the near-misses, the narrowing options. Let the reader hear the dogs barking, radios buzzing, boots getting closer. Have your character throw obstacles behind them, jump from balconies, cut through kitchens, dive into rivers, or leap into a moving car. But don't make them invincible. Let them get grazed. Let them limp. Let them *almost* lose. The thrill comes from the closeness of the threat.

Also play with **camouflage and deception**. Maybe your spy vanishes not by running, but by hiding in plain sight. A janitor's uniform. A food delivery bag. A hijacked surveillance feed that hides their escape route. Give them tools—make-up kits for quick disguise, burner phones to mislead pursuers, signal jammers, forged access cards. Not all escapes have to be fast. Sometimes the best ones are clever, where the protagonist doesn't run at all—they just become invisible.

And when the escape ends, it doesn't really end. The character should still feel hunted. Let them change SIM cards in a bathroom stall. Let them wash blood off their hands in a dirty sink. Let them sleep in a different hotel every night for a week. Escape has a psychological aftermath—paranoia, fatigue, guilt, and sometimes adrenaline addiction. Use those layers to deepen your character.

Your antagonist should also play a role. Were they watching the escape happen? Did they *let* the spy get away? Was the escape expected, part of a bigger trap? Maybe the villain knows your protagonist's tactics and predicts every move. Or maybe this time, your spy pulled a fast one they didn't see coming. Either way, the escape should shift the balance of power. It's not just a breath of relief—it's a reset. The board's been shaken. New alliances may form. New enemies may emerge. And everyone is now aware that someone out there slipped through the net.

Finally, remember the golden rule: the best escape scenes don't feel like action for action's sake. They feel like character-revealing, plot-advancing sequences where the protagonist uses everything they know, everything they carry, and everything they believe to claw their way back into control. And sometimes, it's in these moments—exhausted, wounded, off-balance—that they realize the mission isn't over. It's just begun.

In the next chapter, we'll explore the art of crafting a cover identity—because after the escape, your spy can't just run. They have to disappear into someone else. And if they slip up even once, the next chapter might be their last.

The Art of the Cover Identity

In the world of espionage, the most dangerous weapon isn't a gun or a hidden blade. It's a name that doesn't belong to you. A smile that hides your real thoughts. A profession, a history, a passport that's as fake as the accent you've spent months mastering. This is the art of the cover identity—an essential tool for any spy who plans to infiltrate, observe, or vanish without leaving a trace. And in a political or espionage thriller, it's one of the most fascinating aspects to write, because it isn't just about deception. It's about survival through performance.

The best cover identities are not fantasy—they're rooted in truth. A believable cover is one that's built on habits, routines, and backstories deep enough to withstand pressure. It's not enough for your character to say, "I'm a consultant from Brussels." They have to know the names of the neighborhoods. The slang used in cafés. The politics of the moment. The weather patterns, if necessary. Because in this world, being asked "So where are you from exactly?" can be more dangerous than staring down a gun barrel.

So how do you build a good cover for your character? Start by defining their objective. Why do they need a new identity in the first place? Is it to infiltrate an organization? Blend into a foreign country? Meet someone without being followed? Each goal defines the kind of person they need to become. Ask ChatGPT something like, "Create a deep cover identity for an agent infiltrating a corporate lobbying group in Washington," and you'll get a background that includes a job title, alma mater, previous work history, social media activity, even political leanings. That's the level of detail required to survive scrutiny.

Next, consider what makes the cover *stick*. It has to be easy to live in. If your operative is a trained linguist, make the cover identity a translator or international consultant. If they've worked in tech, maybe they're an IT contractor working on short-term government contracts. When the cover aligns with the character's real skills, it becomes seamless, almost effortless to maintain. It's when the lie overlaps with truth that the mask is hardest to detect.

And don't forget documentation. A forged passport might get you through an airport, but a full identity includes tax records, medical history, social media presence, and credit card trails. Modern counterintelligence doesn't just follow people—it follows data. Ask ChatGPT to list what digital footprints are required for a believable civilian identity in a Western democracy, and you'll understand just how many moving pieces go into staying invisible.

The drama in your story doesn't come just from keeping the identity—it comes from almost losing it. Maybe someone calls your character by the wrong name and they answer anyway. Maybe they run into someone from their past who recognizes their face but not the name. Maybe a child innocently asks them something that shakes the whole façade. The tension in these moments isn't about bullets flying—it's about whether the protagonist can keep a grip on the performance.

A great cover identity also involves *emotional discipline*. Living as someone else takes a toll. Your character might find themselves slipping—starting to believe the lie, or forgetting who they really are. Maybe they've spent so long pretending to be a kindhearted architect that they forget how to handle violence when it comes. Or maybe the opposite—maybe they start to enjoy the lie too much. That tension between who they were, who they are, and who they're pretending to be is a potent narrative thread.

Then there's the challenge of building *relationships* under false pretenses. A spy in deep cover might fall in love, make friends, or form bonds that are entirely based on deception. What happens when those relationships start to feel real? What happens when they have to choose between the mission and the people they've deceived? Use this to deepen your plot. It's not always the enemy who threatens to expose the protagonist—it's the people who care about the identity they've built.

It's also smart to give your character *multiple* identities. One for high-level infiltration. One for escape. One that no one else knows about. Think of these identities like layers of armor. When one fails, they fall back to the next. But with each fall, they lose a piece of themselves. That erosion—the slow unpeeling of names, pasts, habits—is what makes the spy human. And what makes the audience wonder if, by the end, there will be anything left of the original person beneath the masks.

Another powerful angle is when the cover identity is *a trap*. Maybe the antagonist knows the real name behind the face. Maybe someone set up a false identity just to lure the protagonist in. These reversals flip the narrative and force your character to go off script—to survive by instinct, not procedure. Ask ChatGPT for ideas on how a cover identity could be compromised without anyone pulling a gun. The options will surprise you—facial recognition, voice analysis, inconsistent body language. And all of them can build toward a sudden collapse of control.

And don't forget the small tells. Your spy might have an accent they're trying to suppress. A reflex that doesn't match their cover story. A skill they shouldn't have. Maybe they respond too quickly when someone says "Agent." Maybe they pause before answering to their alias. These micro-details add texture to your character's performance—and they give readers those delicious moments of suspense where they know the character is one wrong word away from disaster.

In the end, the cover identity is not just a disguise—it's a crucible. It reveals who your protagonist *really* is through the act of pretending to be someone else. It's a high-wire act, and every minute they live inside it, the fall gets closer. The audience knows it can't last forever. And that ticking tension is where your story lives.

In the next chapter, we'll dive into surveillance, counterintelligence, and tail avoidance—because once your spy is out there, wearing a mask and walking enemy territory, the question isn't just whether they'll complete the mission. It's whether they're already being watched.

Surveillance, Counterintelligence, and Tail Avoidance

In a political or espionage thriller, your protagonist is never alone—even when they think they are. Eyes are always watching. Devices are always listening. And someone, somewhere, is trying to stay one step ahead. Surveillance and counterintelligence are the invisible battlegrounds where spies win or lose everything. The moments when nothing appears to be happening are often the most dangerous. If infiltration is the art of entering unseen, then tail avoidance is the art of staying free. If cover identities protect a spy's face, surveillance tradecraft protects their *moves*.

Modern surveillance is everywhere. CCTV cameras hang from lampposts. Satellites see through cloud cover. Cell phones log locations. Bank cards track movement. Facial recognition software can match you to a photo snapped across the street. It's not just governments running surveillance anymore—it's private companies, security contractors, and even rogue operators. So your spy isn't just avoiding men in black—they're dodging an entire *network*. Writing this convincingly means understanding the tools, and then showing how your character dances between the cracks.

Let's start with **visual surveillance**. In public spaces, cameras are omnipresent. Cities like London and Beijing have millions of them. Your spy knows this. So they might wear clothing that hides facial structure—hoods, glasses, hats—or use facial disruption techniques like reflective materials or asymmetric makeup patterns that confuse recognition software. Maybe they even time their route so they're always in someone else's shadow. They don't move like a normal person—they move with awareness of *where* they're being seen, and *when*.

Now add **human surveillance**—the tail. It might be one person or an entire team working in relays. This is where tradecraft shines. A smart operative never walks in a straight line. They make unpredictable turns. They stop for no reason. They step onto buses and get off one stop later. They go through revolving doors, out the other side, and pause to tie a shoelace while scanning reflections in shop windows. If someone's following, these irregular movements force a tail to make a mistake. One wrong step and the spy knows they've been made.

Use ChatGPT to simulate anti-surveillance techniques. Ask, "Describe a sequence of movements a spy would use to detect if they're being followed through an urban environment," and you'll get a detailed chain of behavior that can be built right into your scenes. The best part? This isn't flashy action—it's subtle tension. The spy sees a shadow in a mirror. A repeated face in a crowd. A man with the same limp who's always one block back. Readers will lean in, trying to spot the tail at the same time as the protagonist.

Then there's **digital surveillance**. Smartphones are tracking devices. Laptops leak data. Smartwatches ping locations. Your spy will know how to turn these off, swap SIM cards, spoof signals, or use Faraday pouches to block wireless transmission. Maybe they use a burner phone that gets destroyed after a single call. Maybe they use encrypted communication tools with one-way wipes. Or maybe, for deep operations, they go full analog—paper maps, hand signals, drop boxes.

But the game goes both ways. Your protagonist isn't just avoiding surveillance—they might be *doing* surveillance. Planting bugs in a hotel room. Tapping a fiber-optic line. Hacking a satellite uplink from a van parked three blocks away. They might trail a suspect using a micro-drone disguised as a bird, or bug a coat pocket with a coin-sized tracker. Ask ChatGPT to list covert surveillance tools and how they're deployed, and you'll open a whole toolbox of dramatic possibilities.

And don't forget **behavioral tells**. A good spy studies movement. They notice when a car behind them doesn't turn after ten blocks. When a barista seems too interested in their name. When a woman holding a baby passes the same street corner three times. They look for inconsistencies in background actors, and they notice the *absence* of normal chaos. If a busy street is too quiet, something's wrong. If a hotel room has fresh towels, but the bed hasn't been touched, someone's been there. These subtle clues say more than any dialogue could.

Your story can heighten suspense by introducing a *tail without revealing it right away*. Let the reader follow the spy through a normal day, while dropping hints. A person in a brown coat shows up again. A van parks across the street. A text message arrives that wasn't supposed to. Maybe the protagonist doesn't notice right away—but the reader does. That dramatic irony puts pressure on the page. The reader wants to shout, "You're being watched!"

Then give your character tools for **counterintelligence**—the art of not just avoiding surveillance, but turning it back on the watcher. Maybe they slip a bug into the tail's jacket. Maybe they lead them into a dead zone and confront them. Or maybe they set a trap, letting themselves be followed just long enough to feed disinformation. The goal isn't always to disappear. Sometimes the best play is to *let* the enemy watch—and manipulate what they see.

Counterintelligence is also political. Maybe a government agency starts tailing your character because of misinformation. Maybe your antagonist frames your protagonist by planting evidence and alerting authorities. Maybe the protagonist is being surveilled by *both* sides, each misinterpreting their actions. This kind of narrative pressure makes every movement feel like a gamble.

And then there's the moment your character *knows* they've been made. Their tail makes eye contact. A message appears where only one person could've left it. A phone vibrates with a single word: **RUN**. From here, the chase begins—or the misdirection deepens. But that realization—that they're being watched—should hit hard. It's not paranoia anymore. It's confirmed. And now the game is no longer about staying hidden. It's about surviving long enough to get ahead.

So when you write surveillance and counter-surveillance scenes, don't think in terms of car chases and sniper scopes. Think about reflection, routine, and rhythm. Think about how to build tension in a conversation where one person knows something the other doesn't. Think about how your character uses space, silence, and misdirection like a magician. And always remember: the best spy stories don't just make readers ask *who's watching*. They make them ask, *who isn't?*

Writing the Twist: When Allies Become Enemies

In the political and espionage thriller, betrayal isn't a twist—it's a tradition. The moment when an ally reveals themselves to be something else entirely is one of the most powerful devices in your toolbox. Done right, it's not just shocking—it's *devastating*. It upends the narrative, wounds the protagonist deeply, and throws every decision, every word, every shared glance into a new and painful light. This is the genre of double-crosses, and when an ally becomes the enemy, the emotional and narrative fallout should be nothing short of seismic.

The key to making this moment work is groundwork. A betrayal that comes out of nowhere might surprise your reader, but a betrayal that, in hindsight, was *always possible*—that's the one that hits hardest. That's the betrayal that earns its place. Which means the character who turns must be believable in both roles: trustworthy enough to lower the hero's guard, and motivated enough to justify the turn. They can't be a plot device. They have to be a person.

Let's start with *who* betrays your protagonist. Is it a long-time partner? A handler? A love interest? A political ally? Each version carries different emotional weight. A betrayal from a colleague might challenge your protagonist's judgment. A betrayal from a mentor might shake their faith. A betrayal from someone they love? That's personal. That leaves scars. Ask ChatGPT to help you sketch a character arc for a double agent posing as a friend, and you'll see how even a few early clues can be seeded without tipping your hand too soon.

The best betrayals come from characters with clear motivations. They're not just "bad now"—they always had a goal that *eventually* conflicted with the protagonist's. Maybe they were working for a rival agency. Maybe they believed in a cause more than in the friendship. Maybe they were protecting someone. Or maybe they weren't who they said they were from the start. The betrayal works when the reader sees it and says, "Of course." Not "Where did that come from?"

One powerful tactic is the *slow reveal*. Maybe the traitor's betrayal isn't an explosion—it's a crack. A missed call. A strange expression. A lie that doesn't match up. Your protagonist begins to doubt—and we, as readers, start doubting with them. Use ChatGPT to generate a list of subtle behavioral cues for a character hiding a second allegiance. That way, the scene builds pressure before the reveal detonates.

Another approach is the *snap betrayal*—where everything collapses in a single, brutal moment. A character draws a gun. A trusted voice gives the kill order. A flash drive handed over turns out to be bait. These twists are fast, brutal, and memorable—but they still require setup. Even in snap betrayals, the signs were there. They just weren't seen.

To add depth, give the betrayer a *moment of truth*. Let them explain why they did it. Let them believe they had no choice. The more human the betrayal, the more it hurts. Maybe they thought the protagonist would understand. Maybe they begged not to be in this position. Or maybe they always envied the hero, and this is payback. Don't make them monologue—make them *bleed*. Emotionally or literally. This is the moment where ideology clashes with loyalty, and you want the audience caught in that crossfire.

Then there's the fallout. A betrayal doesn't end with the twist—it *starts* something new. The hero is rattled. Alone. Cut off. Every safehouse is compromised. Every plan, suddenly suspect. Maybe they were fed false information. Maybe the mission was never what they thought. The betrayal cracks the narrative in half and forces the protagonist to rebuild their purpose with a new understanding of who—and what—they're truly up against.

This twist is also a turning point in your spy's arc. Maybe they become more ruthless. Maybe they start trusting no one. Or maybe they *refuse* to become cold, which makes the next betrayal even riskier. Either way, this moment should change them. They can't walk away from this one unmarked.

And here's where things get really interesting: sometimes the betrayer comes back. Maybe they regret what they did. Maybe they offer to help. Maybe they were undercover so deep that the betrayal was *part* of the mission. Now the protagonist—and the reader—has to decide: are they back for real, or is this another manipulation? That ambiguity keeps tension high and trust nonexistent.

Ask ChatGPT for ideas like: "Give me three possible outcomes after a trusted ally betrays the spy protagonist," and you'll get choices that allow you to steer the story in unpredictable but satisfying ways. Maybe the protagonist forgives them. Maybe they kill them. Maybe they keep them close—just close enough to watch them fall apart.

Remember: in espionage, betrayal isn't rare—it's routine. But that doesn't make it any less personal. In a world of shifting allegiances and buried truths, trust is the rarest resource of all. When an ally becomes an enemy, the real question isn't "how could they do it?" It's "who's next?"

Dead Drops, Black Sites, and Shadow Networks

Beneath the surface of any political or espionage thriller lies a second world—a world of silent communication, hidden detention centers, and invisible allegiances. This isn't the world of clean suits and open warfare. It's the world of whispered messages, hooded prisoners, and favors traded in coded language. Welcome to the backbone of clandestine operations: dead drops, black sites, and shadow networks.

These elements aren't window dressing. They are the infrastructure of the genre—the arteries through which your thriller pulses. They allow spies to communicate without speaking, to vanish without a trace, and to manipulate global events from the shadows. Writing them well means tapping into that layer of reality beneath the official narrative. It means showing readers how information really moves, how people really disappear, and how power is really brokered.

Let's begin with **dead drops**. At their simplest, a dead drop is a way to pass information between operatives without direct contact. It's a rock that's not really a rock. It's a gum wrapper tucked into a specific corner of a bench. It's a book in a library, returned with a slip inside. The genius of a dead drop is in its anonymity. The spy who drops the item never sees the one who picks it up. And in a world where every face and voice can be recorded, that distance is everything.

Dead drops can be physical or digital. A USB stick glued under a toilet tank in a hotel. A burner phone left ringing in a trash bin behind a subway station. Or more subtle: a graffiti mark, a chalk X, a bent blade of grass—signals that the drop is live. Ask ChatGPT to help you come up with a list of dead drop methods used in modern intelligence, and you'll find creative, low-tech solutions that are as clever as they are quiet.

But there's tension in the handoff. Maybe someone else finds the drop first. Maybe it's being watched. Maybe it's a test. In a well-written thriller, a dead drop isn't just an exchange—it's a gamble. And every time your protagonist uses one, they should question who's on the other side. Friend, enemy, or worse: someone pretending to be either.

Now let's move to the darker heart of this world—**black sites**. These are facilities that exist without acknowledgment, hidden from oversight, law, and even geography. They are where governments detain, interrogate, and erase people who can't be officially processed. Your protagonist might be taken to one. Or maybe they're breaking someone *out* of one. Or maybe they just know of its existence—and that knowledge alone puts a target on their back.

Black sites are not just prisons. They're zones of moral erosion. Inside them, truth bends. Loyalties crack. People disappear in layers—name, voice, hope. Writing these locations requires a sense of psychological pressure. Cells without clocks. Light that never turns off. Water that drips forever. Guards who never speak. Maybe your character is in one for a single night—or maybe they spent years in one, and it changed them forever.

Ask ChatGPT to describe the internal layout of a fictional black site operated by a rogue intelligence group, and use that blueprint to shape your scenes. Is it clinical and cold, or industrial and decaying? Does it operate under a false identity—a logistics depot, a research lab, an airfield that's officially decommissioned? These are the places where stories are erased, not told. And if your protagonist survives one, they'll never be the same.

Then there's the lifeblood of the spy world—**shadow networks**. These are informal webs of allies, contacts, double agents, smugglers, hackers, and defectors. People who don't show up on official payrolls. People who owe favors, trade information, or sell secrets. Sometimes your protagonist uses these networks to get a new identity, escape a city, track down a ghost. Sometimes they are part of the network themselves—and sometimes the network turns on them.

What makes shadow networks so compelling is that they exist in every city. That bar in Prague where someone always knows what you need. That fixer in Cairo who can get you across the border—if you don't ask too many questions. That ex-CIA analyst who now sells intelligence to the highest bidder from a hotel room in Bangkok. These characters don't wear badges. They wear scars and smiles. And they make the world feel bigger, more lived-in, more dangerous.

Use ChatGPT to help build these networks. A prompt like, "Create a global network of off-the-books operatives who exchange intelligence through encrypted poetry forums," might give you a truly unique system. Or ask for profiles: "Give me five shadow network contacts in Eastern Europe, each with their own specialty and moral compass." Suddenly, you have a web of relationships ready to come alive on the page.

What ties all of this together—dead drops, black sites, and shadow networks—is the constant question of **trust**. Your protagonist must rely on systems designed to conceal, not reveal. Every message could be bait. Every ally could be an informant. Every extraction could be an ambush. These mechanisms let your character do what needs to be done—but they cost them something every time.

And that's the real value of these tools in your story. Not just logistics. Not just plot mechanics. But emotional and moral complexity. Maybe your character leaves a dead drop—and someone innocent picks it up by mistake. Maybe they trade a name to a contact—and that name ends up in a black site. Maybe they burn a bridge in the shadow network to save themselves—and it comes back years later, needing to be rebuilt.

So when you write these scenes, remember: this is the world your spy *really* lives in. It's not on paper. It's not in official reports. It's in whispers, false names, hand signals, burner phones, vanished records, and untraceable favors. It's the invisible architecture of global espionage, and when your character walks through it, they walk the razor's edge between mission success and moral compromise.

In the next chapter, we'll turn our focus to the antagonist's web—how villains operate within this same underground system, and how their use of these tools reveals who they are, what they want, and how far they're willing to go to win.

Building a Web of Lies, Loyalty, and Leverage

In espionage and political thrillers, the antagonist isn't just a person—it's a system. A force. A presence felt in backroom deals, in encrypted emails, in the whisper between two powerful men no one's ever heard of. And at the center of it all is a web. A tangled, sticky network of lies, loyalty, and leverage—each strand connected to the next with careful intention. The villain pulls a string here, and someone dies over there. That's how this world works. Power isn't about muscle—it's about manipulation.

A great antagonist doesn't operate alone. They surround themselves with assets, loyalists, blackmailed officials, private armies, media figures, and silent allies buried deep in legitimate structures. The villain's true power isn't in what they *do*—it's in what they can make others do. This is the essence of the web. And the best part? It's not always clear where it begins or ends. Even your protagonist might be caught in it without knowing.

Start by deciding what your villain *wants*. Is it power, revenge, ideological purity, global destabilization, or control over a government or corporation? Their desire shapes the architecture of their web. A villain who wants to control a political election might plant assets in media, polling firms, and cyber-infrastructure. A villain who wants to dominate the intelligence landscape might embed moles, sabotage missions, or feed bad intel to rivals. Whatever their aim, the web must be strategic—and invisible until it's too late.

Ask ChatGPT for help building this structure. A prompt like, "Design a covert influence network controlled by a political antagonist," can yield a multi-layered map of how power moves behind the scenes. You'll get ideas like compromised aides, media influencers, ghost accounts, and shell companies, all serving the antagonist without ever meeting them directly. It's all plausible—and terrifying.

Now bring in the **lies**. The antagonist's strength comes from rewriting reality. They control what others believe is true. Maybe they frame your protagonist for a crime they didn't commit. Maybe they leak a story that spins a heroic act into an atrocity. Maybe they falsify intelligence, convincing entire agencies to act against their own interests. These lies aren't wild—they're precise. The best lies are *mostly* true, laced with just enough fiction to steer the narrative.

Consider how these lies shape the world. A forged photo leaked to the press. A doctored audio file. A fake memo passed to a whistle-blower. Let the reader feel the power of these lies—not because they're outlandish, but because they're *believable*. Use ChatGPT to generate disinformation tactics or fake operations designed to discredit someone with surgical efficiency. These details give your villain teeth.

Next, weave in **loyalty**. Who serves this antagonist—and why? Some are true believers, convinced the end justifies the means. Others are paid well to stay quiet. Some are bound by personal debts. Others are trapped—blackmailed, threatened, owned. Not all allies are equal. The key to writing them well is variety. Create a mix of the loyal, the fearful, and the useful. Show us what happens when one tries to leave. Show us how the villain reinforces their loyalty—not just with rewards, but with fear, charm, or ideology.

This is where **leverage** comes in. Your antagonist doesn't need to threaten people directly. They keep files. They watch families. They know about offshore accounts and past mistakes. When they make an offer, it doesn't sound like a threat. It sounds like the only way out. "I can protect you," they say. "But I need something first." Leverage is currency, and your villain spends it sparingly. It's more powerful when it sits in the drawer unopened.

Ask ChatGPT to generate forms of leverage that a high-level antagonist could use over political, military, or intelligence figures. You'll get ideas that feel disturbingly real—hidden affairs, illegal transfers, past affiliations, or family members with secrets. These aren't just background details. They're the threads your villain pulls to get what they want—without ever stepping into the light.

And don't forget that **some of the web might work without the antagonist's direct involvement**. That's the beauty of systems. When your villain builds something smart, it keeps functioning even if they're taken out. A loyal deputy steps in. A dead man's switch activates. A news cycle continues to spin the same story. A shadow network doesn't crumble with one bullet—it resists, adapts, regenerates. That's what makes it dangerous.

Then use this web to *trap your protagonist*. Maybe they think they've found the mole—only to discover the mole was meant to be caught. Maybe they flip someone in the network—only to realize that person was never truly out. Maybe the protagonist breaks into a facility, gets the hard drive, escapes under fire—only to find it was planted with false intel all along. The villain *wanted* them to run with it.

And sometimes, the web tightens unexpectedly. An old friend turns out to be part of it. A source goes quiet. A safehouse is compromised. Not because of sloppiness, but because the villain already knew the plan. This is how you make the antagonist feel omniscient—without ever putting them in the room.

Eventually, your protagonist may start using the same tactics. Spreading their own lies. Flipping assets. Creating leverage. That moral grey area is where the genre thrives. When the hero begins weaving their own web—just to survive—you know the story has matured. Now it's not just about right and wrong. It's about *who controls the truth*.

Political Intrigue: When Power Is the True Weapon

Espionage thrillers love a good chase, a brutal interrogation, or a last-minute extraction under fire—but the sharpest blades are often the ones never drawn. In the world of political thrillers, real danger doesn't come from bullets or bombs. It comes from backroom deals, misdirection, withheld intelligence, and the subtle reshaping of narratives. Political intrigue is the invisible force that manipulates nations, destroys reputations, and topples empires without a single shot being fired. Power, in this context, is the weapon—and the battlefield is perception.

When you write political intrigue well, you force your reader to look past the obvious. You invite them into a world where every smile is strategic, every vote is transactional, and every alliance is temporary. There are no clear heroes—only survivors, opportunists, loyalists, and those caught in the crossfire of a system designed to protect itself at any cost.

The first thing to understand is that **political power is always layered**. It's rarely held by the person at the podium. Instead, it lives in committees, in secretaries, in donors, in advisors with decades of tenure and no public profile. Your antagonist might not be a president or a prime minister. It might be the aide who controls the calendar. The lobbyist who writes the legislation. The agency director who can redact an entire truth with a signature. Use ChatGPT to build out the layers of a fictional government. Ask for profiles of backroom operators—chiefs of staff, intelligence liaisons, corporate influencers—and let those characters shape the real conflict.

Next, understand that **political intrigue is a long game**. No one wins with a single speech or a brilliant checkmate. They win through accumulation—of influence, favors, leverage, secrets. Your characters don't just move pieces on the board. They become part of the board. A senator signs off on a bill that buries funding for a covert op. A diplomat stalls a treaty that prevents foreign intervention. A whistle-blower is quietly reassigned to protect the narrative. It's subtle. It's slow. But it's devastating.

Power in this world is rarely loud. It's quiet confidence. It's the character who controls the next ten moves, not just the current one. Maybe your protagonist wants to expose corruption, but the person they're up against controls the media, the judiciary, and the intelligence community. Maybe every step your hero takes is anticipated, redirected, absorbed by the machine. That's where the tension lives—in watching someone scream into a storm that never answers back.

Political intrigue also means **weaponizing loyalty**. Not just the loyalty of aides and staffers, but the loyalty of the public. The character who controls the story controls the people. Maybe your villain releases a scandal about your protagonist the night before they testify. Maybe they flood the media with half-truths and spin, making the real truth sound like conspiracy. Maybe they leak classified documents not to inform the public—but to *distract* them from something worse. These strategies are quiet warfare. They don't destroy bodies—they destroy credibility.

Ask ChatGPT to create a media manipulation strategy for a corrupt politician trying to neutralize a rogue agent, and you'll get ideas for narrative control, planted leaks, character assassination, and coordinated disinformation campaigns. The villain might not need to pull a trigger—they just need to make the protagonist look unstable, disloyal, or dangerous to the wrong people.

Political intrigue also creates a fertile ground for **betrayals and reversals**. The ally who turns out to be working with the opposition. The rival who suddenly becomes an asset. The enemy who reaches across the divide not out of kindness—but necessity. In this world, nothing is fixed. Power shifts with perception. A single leaked memo can bring down a government. A quiet meeting in a parking garage can change the direction of an entire agency. Let your characters live in that uncertainty, where even trust is transactional.

The emotional payoff comes from **internal conflict**. Maybe your protagonist believed in the system. Maybe they fought to change it. But now they see it for what it is: self-preserving, morally gray, corrupt in places too deep to clean. Do they walk away? Do they fight from within? Do they use the same tools they once condemned? That moral unraveling—watching idealism crash into reality—is where the political thriller gains its true edge.

And sometimes, the most damning revelation isn't a villain's crime—it's the realization that no one cares. That the truth doesn't matter as much as the narrative. That winning the vote matters more than doing the right thing. That the person who holds power will always write the rules—even as they break them.

To write political intrigue convincingly, *slow everything down*. Give characters moments of silence. Let them exchange knowing looks across a conference table. Let dialogue hide more than it reveals. Readers in this genre crave subtext. They want to parse every line, every pause. And when something finally breaks—when someone says the thing they weren't supposed to say—it should feel like a bomb going off in the quietest room in the world.

So let your political players scheme in soft tones and expensive suits. Let the tension come from silence. From the letter that never arrives. The vote that flips. The ally who goes off-script. Because in this world, a whisper can kill faster than a bullet—and when power is the true weapon, the most dangerous person is the one who never seems dangerous at all.

Dialogue That Reveals and Deceives

In a political or espionage thriller, dialogue isn't just about what's said—it's about what's hidden. It's the quiet war between what someone wants you to hear and what they actually mean. Every conversation is a dance of information, power, and misdirection. One line can reveal a betrayal. One word can signal danger. And the best lines don't just move the story forward—they turn it inside out.

In this genre, dialogue has to do double duty. It must reveal character, move the plot, and—most importantly—create *doubt*. Who is telling the truth? Who's playing a role? Who's trying to get the upper hand without ever raising their voice? This is where your spy shows their real weapon: language. Because in this world, bullets are loud, but words are surgical.

Start with **intention**. In every exchange, both characters want something—even if it's just to maintain control. Maybe one wants information. Maybe the other wants to see if they're being followed. Maybe they're testing loyalty, or fishing for a reaction. That's the engine behind every great line of dialogue in a thriller: unspoken objectives. Ask ChatGPT for help building subtext-rich exchanges. A prompt like, "Write a tense dialogue between a spy and their handler where both are hiding something," will give you layered conversations you can shape and refine.

The best scenes are filled with **veiled language**. Characters speak in code. Not always formal codes or passwords, but carefully chosen phrases that carry weight only if you know the context. "It's going to rain tomorrow," might mean the operation is a go. "Did you see the fireworks last night?" could mean surveillance has been compromised. You don't have to explain it in the moment. Let the reader feel that something's off—then deliver the payoff later. That retroactive realization makes for thrilling fiction.

Then you've got **misdirection**—the lies spoken so well they sound like truths. Your characters should be good at pretending. A spy might give just enough truth to make the lie believable. They might smile while lying. They might stall with a story that sounds real because it *is*, except for one key detail. Let your reader play detective. Let them wonder what's real. And when the reveal finally comes, let it reframe everything that was said earlier.

One way to make dialogue razor-sharp is to **strip it down**. The best lines in this genre are often short. Clipped. Loaded. A well-placed "I know who you are" can hit harder than a paragraph of threats. Silence is powerful too. A pause. A look. The absence of a response. Sometimes the tension comes not from what's said, but from what *isn't* said.

You can also weaponize **contrast**. A cheerful tone paired with a deadly threat. A friendly conversation laced with menace. Two enemies chatting like old friends while secretly plotting to kill each other. Or two allies speaking cautiously because they're being listened to. These contrasts keep the reader off-balance, always questioning the scene's true purpose.

And don't forget the **interrogation-style exchange**. These aren't always in a basement with a spotlight overhead. They happen in cafes, on park benches, during elevator rides. One person is probing. The other is deflecting. The pace is fast, the answers rehearsed. Use ChatGPT to generate questions an intelligence officer might ask when unsure of someone's allegiance. Mix those in with personal or disarming questions, and you'll create a rhythm that feels authentic and dangerous.

Use dialogue to *challenge* your characters. Let someone say the one thing that gets under the spy's skin. Let them bring up a past mission, a personal failure, a moral compromise. Dialogue isn't just a tool—it's a weapon. Characters should use it to wound, test, provoke, seduce, and, when necessary, manipulate.

Sometimes, a character says something they *shouldn't*. Maybe they reveal a detail they couldn't possibly know. Maybe they say a name your protagonist never mentioned. These slips are gold. A single wrong word can unravel an entire lie. And when your character catches it—when they realize they've been talking to the enemy all along—it shifts the whole scene. These small missteps can explode into major plot turns if placed carefully.

And always let your protagonist **read between the lines**. Give them dialogue cues to react to—faltering tone, evasive eyes, stammered corrections. Let them ask themselves, *Why did they say it that way? What aren't they saying?* This not only builds suspense, it gives the audience a front-row seat to the spy's greatest tool: intuition sharpened by years in the shadows.

Lastly, let your dialogue *echo*. Let lines come back later in new contexts. A phrase that once meant safety could now signal betrayal. A compliment could have been a veiled threat all along. Repetition, when done right, isn't lazy—it's chilling. It makes the world feel connected. And it reminds the reader that in this genre, nothing said is ever just what it seems.

Writing Diplomatic Tension that Feels Like a Knife Fight

Diplomacy in a political or espionage thriller isn't polite conversation over tea. It's war by other means. The language is formal, but the stakes are fatal. The smiles are practiced, but the eyes are scanning for weakness. And beneath every word, there's a threat not yet spoken. Writing diplomatic tension is about turning a meeting room into a battlefield, where every pause, every handshake, every phrase has weight. When done right, it should feel like a knife fight—silent, precise, and just one slip away from blood on the floor.

The first thing to understand is that **diplomatic scenes are power struggles in slow motion**. Everyone at the table wants something. No one says what they really mean. And everyone is trying to walk away with more than they came in with. Your job is to create a scenario where the stakes are hidden but unmistakably high—where a single misstep could spark a war, leak a secret, or expose an alliance that was never meant to see daylight.

Think of diplomacy in thriller fiction as a form of chess. Characters are playing moves ahead. Maybe it's a summit between two hostile nations, a closed-door negotiation in a private embassy, or a U.N. session with side conversations that matter more than the main event. The trick is to keep the reader tuned in to what *isn't* being said. Use ChatGPT to help map out motives, weaknesses, and hidden agendas for each side. A prompt like, "Outline three conflicting goals of participants in a high-stakes peace negotiation," can give you fuel for subtext-rich conversations and tight scenes.

Every good diplomatic exchange in this genre operates on **three levels**: the surface conversation, the subtext, and the unspoken threat. On the surface, two officials might be discussing a trade deal. But underneath, one knows the other has been funding rebels. And both know that if the deal falls through, the military buildup on the border won't stay theoretical. The dialogue isn't filler—it's theater, with every line designed to keep control or provoke a mistake.

The real thrill comes when **tension seeps through the cracks of civility**. Maybe a smile lingers too long. Maybe someone responds to a hypothetical with too much knowledge. Maybe someone "accidentally" refers to a country by its old name—a subtle political insult that sets the room on fire. Use these moments to remind the reader that beneath the tailored suits and marble conference tables, everyone's carrying a blade.

Writing this kind of scene well means focusing on **precision of language**. Let characters speak in statements that sound generous, but come with conditions. "We're open to dialogue" might mean "We'll listen while your country bleeds." "Let's not escalate" could mean "You've already gone too far." Let readers feel the breath-holding between lines. The sense that every word might be used as evidence later.

Body language matters, too. A diplomatic scene should be filled with tension that doesn't need to be spoken. Someone pours tea too slowly. Someone doesn't rise to shake hands. A note passed under the table changes the entire mood. A journalist watching the event catches none of this—but your reader does. Let them live in that inner circle of perception, where the real meaning happens in glances, silences, and minor missteps.

And let your **protagonist feel the pressure**. If they're in the room, maybe they're representing a country. Or maybe they're watching their superior try to contain a crisis. Maybe they see a moment of opportunity and use it to steer the conversation off-course. Or maybe they make a mistake—speak too soon, offer too much, misread the subtext—and feel the mood shift like a blade to the throat. These scenes work best when you remember that diplomacy isn't safety. It's *calculated risk*.

You can even layer in **external tension**. Maybe a diplomatic meeting is unfolding while a covert op is in progress. One side speaks of peace while their agents plant listening devices. One delegate praises unity while outside, protesters clash with police. The scene becomes a metaphor—calm words balancing on top of chaos, and the reader knows one feeds the other.

The other essential tool in this scene is **leverage**. Who has it, who wants it, and who's bluffing about it. Maybe one side has intel the other doesn't know they have. Maybe someone in the room is secretly recording everything for blackmail. Maybe an ambassador has been compromised by the opposition and is playing both sides. You can use ChatGPT to brainstorm sources of leverage in diplomatic settings—economic, political, personal. These stakes turn words into weapons.

Also, don't be afraid to **break decorum at just the right moment**. A character slamming a glass, walking out of a negotiation, letting an insult slip—it snaps the tension and tells the reader: the gloves are off. That's the moment the knife fight goes from metaphor to reality. That's the shift from diplomacy to escalation, and your readers will feel it in their gut.

A good diplomatic scene doesn't end with an agreement. It ends with *something changing*. A new threat. A quiet alliance. A lie exposed. A truth accepted in silence. Let the aftermath ripple through your story. Maybe a war starts later, but it started *here*, at this table, with this smile, with this denial. That's the beauty of political thrillers—violence is only one kind of danger. Language, reputation, alliances—these are just as deadly, and far harder to undo.

Pacing the Thriller: Action, Interrogation, Revelation

Pacing is everything in a political or espionage thriller. It's the pulse beneath the surface, the rhythm that controls when your reader breathes—and when they hold that breath without realizing it. Unlike straightforward action genres, pacing in this kind of thriller is about *precision*. You're managing silence and chaos, control and collapse, planning and panic. And the secret to doing it well is knowing when to unleash movement, when to slow down, and when to rip the curtain off and show something nobody was supposed to see.

There are three anchors that define the pace of your story: **action**, **interrogation**, and **revelation**. Each one serves a different purpose, but they all work together to maintain tension. Think of them like turns in a screw. You tighten with interrogation, release with action, and twist the knife with revelation. Let's break each one down and look at how they feed the heartbeat of your thriller.

Start with **action**. Not just fight scenes or chase sequences—action means momentum. It's the *movement* of the plot. It's when the character decides to follow someone, break into a facility, or flee from a double-cross. When well-written, action scenes don't just get the heart racing—they get the story moving. And pacing-wise, they act as punctuation marks. They snap the reader awake. They signal that things are accelerating, even if the characters don't yet understand why.

You don't need nonstop violence to keep action in your story. A footstep behind the protagonist in a parking garage. A dropped phone. A missed text. A moment where everything slows—and then explodes. Let the action be *earned*. Let it feel like an inevitable result of all the lies and moves that came before. And once you've dropped your character into the chaos, don't drag the scene out too long. Let them run. Let them fight. Let them survive. Then pull back—because if everything is high-stakes all the time, nothing feels urgent.

Once action shakes the story, it's time for **interrogation**—the pressure cooker. This is where you slow the pace down, but increase the tension. Interrogation doesn't always mean a prisoner in a chair. It means pressure. Questions. Mental duels. It could be a journalist grilling a government official. A diplomat pinning a spy with veiled accusations. A former friend suddenly asking questions they shouldn't know to ask. These scenes stretch time. They're about control. Who holds the upper hand? Who slips?

Ask ChatGPT to help generate psychological interrogation strategies for spies trained to manipulate or resist—then use that as the foundation for dialogue that feels like a mental sparring match. In terms of pacing, interrogation scenes slow everything down just enough to let the reader squirm. These scenes aren't resting points—they're moments of coiled tension. Someone's trying to crack the story open. The other person's trying to hold it together.

Then you hit the **revelation**—the twist, the truth, the moment that changes the rules. This is the narrative turn where the reader learns something the characters didn't—or the protagonist uncovers a secret that reframes the entire mission. This could be a betrayal, a discovered mole, a coded message decoded, or a body turning up that shouldn't. Pacing-wise, revelations are emotional spikes. They don't require movement or bullets. They require clarity. You don't need to rush them. In fact, the best ones arrive in silence. Let the character realize what it means. Let the weight of the truth settle before the next move is made.

A revelation, followed by inaction—*that's* where the pacing tightens. It forces your character to make choices under pressure. Do they expose the truth? Do they keep it secret? Do they trust anyone with it? These moments move the plot forward not with speed, but with gravity. And when used between your bursts of action and interrogation, they hold the reader in a tight loop of suspense.

So how do you balance these three elements?

You **open with a jolt**—a discovery, a death, a chase, or a quiet violation of routine. Then you **pause with an interrogation**—someone needs to explain something, or cover up something, or figure something out. Then you **twist with a revelation**—an answer that wasn't expected. Then you build pressure again. Maybe another action beat. Or another interrogation, but this time more desperate. And you do it all again. Over and over. But tighter each time.

This isn't a roller coaster. It's a spiral. A tightening loop where every rotation costs more. More danger, more lies, more risk. And at the center of the spiral is the truth your protagonist doesn't want to face—about themselves, the system, the people they thought they could trust.

Ask ChatGPT to generate pacing charts for thrillers, and you'll see how story beats often line up like pressure waves. The closer you get to the climax, the shorter the distance between action, interrogation, and revelation. That's how you make a story that feels like it's speeding up, even when it's just getting more intense.

Also, remember the role of **silence** in pacing. Some of the best tension comes in the stillness after the action. A room full of diplomats who've just heard something they weren't supposed to. A spy sitting alone in a hotel room, bleeding and unsure who to trust. A quiet moment where someone realizes they've been betrayed, and all the noise cuts out. That's how pacing controls *feeling*. Let the silence sting.

Your job as the writer is to control the rhythm. To push when the reader gets comfortable. To slow down when the panic rises. To time every reveal so it lands like a punch, and every lull so it loads the next punch with dread.

Using ChatGPT to Build Conspiracy Threads

Conspiracy is the lifeblood of espionage and political thrillers. It's what breathes beneath the surface, behind the headlines, in the footnotes of history. A good conspiracy thread doesn't just serve the plot—it *is* the plot. It fuels paranoia, pushes your protagonist deeper into the shadows, and twists the reader's sense of who is really pulling the strings. Writing conspiracy well means planting false leads, layering truths within lies, and building a web so intricate it feels like it could exist in our own world. And with ChatGPT, you've got a silent co-conspirator who never sleeps.

When using ChatGPT to build conspiracy threads, the first step is deciding your **core deception**. At the heart of every conspiracy is a secret—something dangerous, something denied, something protected at all costs. It might be a covert operation gone wrong, a clandestine surveillance program, a fabricated war, or a rigged election. Your protagonist might stumble onto it by accident—or be assigned to cover it up. Use ChatGPT to brainstorm options with a prompt like: *"Give me ten conspiracy ideas involving government, military, corporate, or media institutions."* From there, you can choose the seed of your plot.

Once you have your core, you need to **bury it under layers**. Conspiracies thrive on complexity. They rely on redundancy. Discredit one piece, and another takes its place. Use ChatGPT to help create tiers within your conspiracy—people who know part of the truth, others who think they're helping, and a few who are pulling strings no one even sees. Ask for hierarchies, cell structures, or compartmentalized operatives who only know the surface of the operation. The deeper your character digs, the more unsettling it becomes.

Your next tool is the **cover story**. For every conspiracy to survive, there must be a believable alternative narrative. The plane crash was an accident. The whistleblower was mentally unstable. The missing file never existed. Use ChatGPT to generate these narratives: *"Write a government press release covering up an unauthorized drone strike,"* or *"Create a media report that spins a covert assassination as a gang-related incident."* These artificial truths give your story a chilling realism. They feel familiar. They feel *plausible*. And that's what makes them dangerous.

From here, you build **clues and breadcrumbs**. Conspiracies in fiction need to unfold in fragments. A redacted document. A photo with a face blurred just enough. A phone call cut off mid-sentence. Ask ChatGPT to help create evidence—fake emails, declassified files, code names for operations. Try: *"Give me a classified memo from a shadow intelligence group approving a secret surveillance campaign in a friendly country."* These details act like connective tissue. The reader begins to follow the same trail your protagonist does, and the tension builds as the full picture emerges.

A good conspiracy also has **conflicting perspectives**. One character believes in the system. One is disillusioned. One is profiting. One wants to destroy it all. Use ChatGPT to write dialogue between these characters, or to build dossiers on the players involved. A prompt like, *"Create character profiles for three insiders who each have a different reason for participating in a massive political cover-up,"* gives you more than just backstory—it gives you tension. Every time these characters interact, the reader can feel the cracks.

And don't forget to create **rabbit holes**. Every conspiracy needs misdirection. Dead ends. False villains. ChatGPT is great at generating these. Try: *"Give me five red herrings that could lead the protagonist away from the real conspiracy for at least 50 pages."* Maybe one of the leads is *partially* true. Maybe one of the enemy agents turns out to be a scapegoat. Maybe someone gets too close to the truth—and disappears.

The beauty of a well-constructed conspiracy is that **it turns the world upside down**. Institutions that once seemed safe—governments, news agencies, international watchdogs—now feel infected. Your protagonist is no longer sure who to trust, and neither is the reader. With ChatGPT, you can keep expanding the scope as needed. When you're stuck, ask it: *"What's the next twist that could make this conspiracy feel even larger and more global?"*

But conspiracies in thrillers aren't just puzzles. They're personal. They change people. Maybe your protagonist was once a loyal servant of the system. But now? Now they see it from the inside—and they're shattered by it. ChatGPT can help you develop this arc. Ask: *"How would a former intelligence officer react emotionally after realizing they helped build a cover-up operation?"* That transformation is what gives your conspiracy weight. It's not just about uncovering a truth. It's about surviving it.

And finally, when it's time to **pull the curtain back**, ChatGPT can help you *dramatize the reveal*. The final report. The confrontation with the traitor. The leak that triggers global outrage. Ask for scene structure, press conference dialogue, or a climactic showdown between the hero and the architect of the conspiracy. Let the reader feel the full force of the truth landing like a grenade.

In a world where reality often feels stranger than fiction, a well-crafted conspiracy thriller doesn't just entertain—it resonates. It plays on our deepest suspicions, our fear that the truth is always just out of reach. And with ChatGPT helping you build the threads, plant the clues, and spin the lies, you don't just write a story.

You build a world where no one is safe—and everything is connected.

Plotting a Global Crisis One Thread at a Time

A global crisis doesn't begin with an explosion—it begins with a whisper. One data breach. One border skirmish. One missing scientist. And from there, the world begins to shift. Markets tremble, alliances fray, and shadows stretch longer across every capital city. In an espionage or political thriller, the global crisis isn't a singular event. It's a web—carefully spun, each thread connected to the next, and when one is pulled, the whole structure begins to vibrate. The trick to writing a compelling global crisis isn't scale—it's *construction*. And with the right approach, you can build a crisis that feels real, urgent, and terrifyingly close.

Start small. The foundation of a great global crisis is a single **instigating incident**—a targeted cyberattack on a power grid, a diplomatic envoy disappearing en route to a summit, a leak of top-secret files revealing illegal covert ops. Ask ChatGPT to generate ideas for plausible but catastrophic triggers: *"Give me ten inciting incidents that could lead to a modern-day international crisis."* The more specific the spark, the more believable the fire that follows.

Once you have your spark, think in **threads**. A global crisis is never caused by one thing—it's the result of interconnected actions, reactions, and manipulations across borders. One country reacts to the leak with sanctions. Another accelerates troop movements near a disputed territory. A third pulls out of an intelligence-sharing agreement. Meanwhile, corporate interests panic, currencies destabilize, and the press spins its own version of the truth. Each of these threads needs its own arc, its own consequences, and—ideally—a character or faction driving it.

Use ChatGPT to help build this geopolitical web. Try prompts like: *"Outline how a leaked arms deal between two hostile nations could destabilize five other countries,"* or *"Describe the economic ripple effects of a false flag operation that blames a neutral country for a cyberattack."* You'll start to see how a crisis builds through influence, blame, reaction, and misinformation.

Then bring in **factions with competing agendas**. A crisis becomes thrilling when not everyone wants to solve it the same way. Maybe one country sees opportunity in the chaos and fans the flames. Maybe an intelligence agency wants to exploit the instability for their own gain. Maybe your protagonist's own government is hiding the fact that they *caused* the crisis in the first place. This is where political, military, and corporate interests collide—and no one's telling the full truth.

Create characters to represent each of these perspectives. Let ChatGPT help design a rogue general, a media-savvy diplomat, a whistleblower, a multinational CEO who profits from war. Each of these characters adds complexity, and each can be a potential ally, threat, or twist in the plot.

Now you're ready to **layer the crisis in acts**.

Act I is confusion. The inciting event happens. The world doesn't yet realize how deep the problem goes. Your protagonist is investigating something that seems small—a document, a murder, a surveillance anomaly.

Act II is escalation. Protests erupt. Satellites are repositioned. Emergency summits are held. Your protagonist starts connecting the threads and realizing the crisis isn't random—it's being manipulated.

Act III is collapse or prevention. The world teeters. Your character must make a decision—reveal the truth and risk global fallout, or suppress it to maintain a fragile order. Maybe they stop a war. Maybe they fail, and a new world order rises from the ashes.

Ask ChatGPT to help you structure each act. Try: *"Create a three-act structure for a thriller where an energy crisis sparks a worldwide diplomatic collapse."* The AI can help you define key moments, transitions, and character decisions that move the story forward while building dread.

Another powerful tool? **Misinformation**. A true global crisis isn't just about actions—it's about *perception*. Maybe the real cause is unknown, but conspiracy theories flood the airwaves. Maybe media outlets report conflicting stories, and no one knows who to believe. Ask ChatGPT to generate headlines, social media chatter, or government statements that reflect different sides of the same crisis. You'll give your world depth—and keep your reader guessing.

Don't forget the **human cost**. In a global thriller, it's easy to get lost in the macro view—treaties, leaders, war rooms. But the reader needs to feel the crisis *on the ground*. Show the refugee crossing a sealed border. The mother searching for formula in a blacked-out city. The young soldier deployed under false pretenses. This is where your story finds heart. Ask ChatGPT for vignettes from different countries experiencing the same event. Let your reader see the crisis from multiple eyes—and fear what comes next.

Finally, the best global crises feel eerily **plausible**. Use current trends and technologies—AI weapon systems, climate migration, deepfake diplomacy, collapsing trade deals—and twist them just slightly. Ask ChatGPT, *"How could a real-world technology be used to simulate a geopolitical incident?"* You'll get ideas grounded in reality, and that's what gives your thriller its bite.

Plotting a global crisis thread by thread isn't about size. It's about tension. It's about watching small decisions become impossible to take back. It's about the slow collapse of order while your protagonist races to uncover the one truth that could stop it all. Or the one truth they might not be allowed to reveal.

Using History and Headlines to Inspire Your Fiction

In the world of political and espionage thrillers, nothing is more powerful—or more terrifying—than a story that feels like it could really happen. That feeling doesn't come from wild imagination alone. It comes from anchoring your fiction in truth. Whether it's pulled from yesterday's headline or a buried historical episode few people remember, real events offer the scaffolding for a story that resonates. The best thrillers don't just entertain—they haunt. And the way you make your story linger in the reader's mind is by rooting it in something they already *know*, even if they don't know why.

Using history and headlines doesn't mean writing a documentary. You're not obligated to get every detail exact. What you're doing is **mirroring reality just closely enough** that the reader wonders if the story is fiction at all. That tension—between what's real and what might be—is where conspiracy breathes, where power becomes personal, and where your plot finds traction.

Let's start with **history**. Political thrillers thrive on long shadows—wars fought in secret, treaties signed behind closed doors, operations that were quietly erased from public record. Dig into Cold War espionage. Look at the coups orchestrated by intelligence agencies. Study the proxy wars of the 20th century. Many of these real-world events are stranger than fiction. The CIA's MKUltra mind control experiments. Operation Ajax in Iran. The Glomar Explorer's secret mission to recover a sunken Soviet sub. These are goldmines for fictional inspiration.

Use ChatGPT as a research tool. Ask, *"List lesser-known intelligence operations from the 1970s that could inspire a modern thriller,"* or *"Give me historical examples of political cover-ups involving multiple nations."* The AI can dig up story seeds that you can replant in new soil. A long-forgotten scandal can be reborn as a modern conspiracy. A defunct black site becomes the setting for your climax. A historical defector becomes a myth within your fictional intelligence community.

But the key to using history isn't replication—it's *reinterpretation*. You're not writing about Watergate. You're writing about a fictional data breach that feels eerily familiar. You're not retelling the fall of the Berlin Wall—you're imagining what happens when a modern wall goes up, digitally, cutting nations off from truth. Take the structure, the tone, the paranoia—and turn it into something new.

Then there are **headlines**—today's stories, already tinged with fear, already whispered about in terms of what's not being said. Cyberattacks. Mysterious deaths of whistleblowers. Leaked classified material. The rise of AI in military applications. Elections swayed by misinformation. These are not plot devices—they're *prototypes*. Your job is to ask: *What if this went further? What if this wasn't the full story? What if this was just the beginning?*

Use ChatGPT to stay current. A prompt like, *"Summarize three current news stories that could be expanded into a political thriller subplot,"* will give you a starting point for scenes or setups. A diplomatic standoff today could be the spark for your novel's global crisis. A corporate scandal this month might become a motive for murder in your screenplay.

You can also ask ChatGPT to **fictionalize** current events: *"Create a fictional scenario based on recent tensions between global superpowers, suitable for a thriller."* This lets you abstract the real event just enough to avoid predictability—and legal trouble—while still keeping the feeling of authenticity.

Another approach is to combine **historical events with current technology**. What if the Watergate burglars had facial recognition to deal with? What if the Iran-Contra affair was hidden behind AI-generated deepfakes? What if Cold

War defectors could've been tracked with smartphone metadata? These mashups allow you to ground your thriller in historical tension while updating the mechanics for a modern audience.

Your protagonist can reflect this duality. Maybe they're a modern spy haunted by the failures of the past. Maybe they're trying to prevent a crisis that mirrors one from their own childhood—or their parent's classified career. That intergenerational connection deepens the stakes and lets you draw parallels between what's changed and what never really has.

Also consider **what's hidden within history and headlines**. Look at what's not being reported. Ask ChatGPT to help you identify gaps: *"What parts of this event are most unclear or unexplained?"* Often, it's not what we know—it's what we *almost* know that makes the best thriller fuel. An empty line in a declassified file. A suspicious coincidence. A public figure who vanished after a scandal and never resurfaced.

You can even create your own **alternative history timeline**, subtly altering one real event and building a fictional world around it. Ask, *"What would the geopolitical consequences be if the Cuban Missile Crisis had ended in military conflict?"* or *"How might the modern world look if a whistleblower had successfully exposed a government's surveillance program in the early 2000s?"* These exercises create a backdrop for rich, believable stories where fiction becomes a plausible version of reality.

The goal in using history and headlines isn't to retell the news—it's to tap into the **emotional truth** that lives beneath it. The fear of not knowing what's real. The anger at being lied to. The helplessness of watching systems fail. The suspicion that the most important decisions are being made in rooms we'll never see.

And when you use that truth as your foundation, your fiction gains weight. It becomes more than just a story—it becomes a *warning*. A whisper in the dark that says, "This could happen. Maybe it already has."

Making Your Thriller Feel Uncomfortably Real

The most haunting thrillers don't explode—they simmer. They don't rely on spectacle—they work in whispers, slow dread, and quiet revelations that feel just close enough to home. When a thriller feels *uncomfortably real*, it seeps into the reader's mind long after the final page. It makes them second-guess headlines, side-eye government statements, and wonder how much of your story is fiction—and how much is warning.

To make your thriller uncomfortably real, you must embrace **plausibility over flash**. Espionage isn't always about secret bunkers and rooftop chases. It's about quiet betrayals, confidential documents sent to the wrong inbox, silences during phone calls that go on just a beat too long. Grounding your story in the rhythm of real-world tension is what makes it linger. You don't need a thousand bodies. You need one man found dead with a USB in his sock—and a government that won't say a word about it.

Start with **what readers already know**. Most people are familiar with the feeling that not everything is being told. That institutions aren't entirely transparent. That power, wherever it concentrates, tends to bend truth for convenience. Your thriller should tap into those *simmering suspicions*. Use current technology, familiar environments, and recognizable authority structures to build the illusion of normalcy—then begin to warp it, just slightly. When the everyday turns sinister, readers pay attention.

Ask ChatGPT to help you create subtle but credible tension in mundane settings. Try: *"Describe a routine government meeting where one detail doesn't feel right and begins to unravel a conspiracy."* The goal isn't drama—it's *discomfort*. Make the reader feel like they've stumbled onto something. Something they weren't supposed to see.

The characters are just as crucial. Your protagonist shouldn't be a superhero. Make them **ordinary in background, exceptional in instinct**. A mid-level analyst, a disillusioned diplomat, a freelance journalist with too much access and too little protection. These characters are easier for readers to relate to because they live on the edge of the world they're investigating. They're not meant to be heroes. They become one only because they *have to*.

Give your protagonist **human limitations**. Let them lose track of things. Let their hands shake. Let them say the wrong thing in a high-stakes conversation. The more grounded they feel, the more terrifying it is when the weight of the plot starts crushing them. ChatGPT can help you build psychological profiles based on stress reactions or trauma history. Ask: *"How would an untrained civilian react to being hunted by intelligence agencies?"* Use the response to inform subtle emotional detail that makes your scenes breathe.

Then, there's **technology**—not fantasy tech, but the things we use every day: smartphones, surveillance cameras, key fobs, public Wi-Fi, facial recognition. Twist them. Let the character realize their own devices are betraying them. Let a smartwatch become a listening device. Let a home assistant start responding to things it wasn't asked. These moments don't need to be loud—they need to be *quietly horrifying*. Try: *"Give me five ways a smart device in a home could be used to monitor or manipulate a spy thriller protagonist without their knowledge."*

A thriller feels real when the enemy is **faceless**. Not a single villain with a speech and a master plan, but an institution, a system, a shadow. Maybe your antagonist is an entire agency that claims to protect the nation. Maybe it's a corporation that owns too much data. Maybe it's an unnamed council of decision-makers who rewrite policy while the world sleeps. The less your villain shouts, the more terrifying they become. The sense of *absence* is what gives power its real weight.

Another strategy is to incorporate **real-world timelines**. Set your thriller in the near future. Or now. Reference events readers know—pandemics, political unrest, trade disputes—and build your fiction in the cracks. If the reader feels like they've *already* seen your world on the news, they'll never quite shake it. Ask ChatGPT: *"Outline a thriller plot set one year after a global energy crisis caused by a cyberattack on power infrastructure."* You'll get a world that feels familiar, but laced with dread.

Use **dialogue** to pull readers in deeper. Keep it clipped. Professional. But let moments slip. Let a character say something that suggests they've seen worse. Let someone admit that the truth doesn't matter—perception does. Let a low-ranking aide hint that what's in the official report isn't the full story. These glimpses of a wider, hidden reality create that itchy sensation that something bigger is happening, and no one is safe from it.

Finally, remember that realism comes from **consequences**. If a journalist leaks information, they lose their job. If an agent goes rogue, they're disavowed. If a protest breaks out, it ends in violence—not cinematic heroism. And sometimes, the protagonist doesn't win. They just *survive*. Let the end of your thriller reflect the real world's grey morality. Maybe the truth gets buried. Maybe the villain walks free. Or maybe your character stops caring about saving the world and starts just trying to protect the people they love.

A thriller that feels uncomfortably real doesn't need to scream to be heard. It needs to whisper something that readers can't "unhear". Something that stays with them the next time they look at a CCTV camera or skim the news. Something that says, "This isn't fiction. Not entirely."

Espionage Ethics: Lies, Betrayal, and the Greater Good

Every political or espionage thriller eventually hits a point where the bullets stop flying, the chase slows down, and something heavier begins to settle on the protagonist's shoulders. It's not fear. It's not regret. It's the question that underpins the entire genre: *Was it worth it?* Espionage is not a clean business. It's built on secrets, deception, manipulation, and sacrifice. And every decision your protagonist makes echoes through the moral architecture of the story. To make your thriller compelling, you need to explore not just *what* your characters do—but *why*, and *what it costs them*.

The ethics of espionage aren't written in black and white. They're painted in a thousand shades of gray. And your job as the writer isn't to hand out judgment—it's to create the circumstances where readers are forced to wrestle with it. What does it mean to lie for the right reasons? When is betrayal justified? Who decides what the "greater good" really is?

Let's start with **lies**. In a spy's world, lying isn't a skill—it's survival. Your protagonist likely lives multiple lives. They lie to enemies, to allies, and often to the people they love the most. They may lie to themselves just to keep moving forward. But when does the lie become who they are? When does the performance stop being an act?

Ask ChatGPT to help explore this in internal monologue. A prompt like, *"Write a reflection by a deep-cover agent who can no longer remember their real name,"* can help you craft those chilling moments of identity erosion. The most devastating lies aren't about operations. They're personal. "I'll come home." "I'm not in danger." "You can trust me." Those are the ones that break something inside.

Then comes **betrayal**—the core of most spy fiction. Betraying a friend, a partner, a cause, or a code. Sometimes betrayal is strategic. Sometimes it's desperate. Sometimes it's simply the only way out. But it's never clean. Let your protagonist make a choice that saves lives but costs someone else everything. Let them give up a contact to protect a mission. Let them burn an asset they promised to protect. Let them do what has to be done—and *feel it* afterward.

Ask ChatGPT to help sketch these moments: *"Describe a scene where a spy must betray their handler to stop a greater threat."* Don't make it easy. Let the dialogue shake. Let the silence stretch. Let the moment stay unresolved. That's how real espionage ethics work—not in victory, but in compromise.

And then, **the greater good**—the phrase that justifies the whole operation. But who defines it? Is it the agency? The government? The individual agent in the field? One of the great ethical dilemmas of espionage fiction is whether the end really justifies the means. Can kidnapping, torture, blackmail, or even assassination ever be moral if it prevents war? Your story becomes most powerful when it asks that question without offering easy answers.

You can use ChatGPT to simulate different perspectives: *"Give me three opposing views from intelligence operatives about whether collateral damage is ever acceptable."* Use these contrasting voices in your dialogue, your arguments, your turning points. Let your characters debate it—then be forced to act before they find peace with their answer.

Also, consider the **personal cost**. Maybe your protagonist used to believe in the greater good. But after years in the field, it feels hollow. They've lost friends. They've lied too often. They've watched innocent people pay the price for the games of powerful men. Maybe now they question everything. Or maybe they've learned to compartmentalize, burying morality under necessity. That emotional drift becomes the heart of the character arc—and often the most resonant part of the story.

Let your thriller explore *empathy as a liability*. Maybe the protagonist connects with someone they're supposed to manipulate. Maybe they start asking questions they're not supposed to. That internal war between duty and conscience is where the ethical tension lives. It's not about being good or bad—it's about *being honest about what it takes to survive in a dishonest world.*

There's also the question of **collateral damage**. The civilians. The pawns. The people who never signed up for any of this. Maybe a surveillance op ruins a family. Maybe a car bomb kills the wrong person. Maybe a journalist gets too close and dies because your character didn't warn them in time. Let these moments change things. Let your character carry that weight. Let the reader feel that this isn't a video game. Every move has consequences.

You can also explore **institutional ethics**. Maybe the agency your character works for used to stand for something. Maybe now it's just a machine. What happens when a character starts to realize the system they serve is no longer what they thought it was? Maybe they go rogue. Maybe they try to fix it from within. Maybe they realize *they're* the villain in someone else's story. Use ChatGPT to flesh out these crises of loyalty: *"Write a scene where a field agent confronts their superior over a mission that cost innocent lives."*

The truth is, most espionage thrillers don't end with peace. They end with silence. With a character sitting alone, wondering if the mission they completed actually made anything better. That's what makes this genre different. It's not about saving the world. It's about choosing who pays the price.

So lean into the discomfort. Let the reader feel like they don't know what side they're on. Let them see the lies that kept the peace. Let them meet the people betrayed in the name of stability. And when your protagonist finally walks away from it all—if they can—let them ask the only question that really matters: *Was it worth it?*

The Mole in the System: Internal Betrayal

If espionage is built on lies, then the most dangerous lie of all is the one that sits beside you in the same office, wears the same uniform, speaks the same mission language—and slowly poisons everything from the inside. The mole isn't just a character. It's a virus in the bloodstream of your story. It breeds paranoia. It unravels trust. And in a well-constructed political or espionage thriller, the mole doesn't just complicate the plot—they *redefine* it.

Internal betrayal shifts the tone of your narrative. It forces your protagonist to stop looking outward and start questioning their own environment—possibly even themselves. The real tension isn't in the reveal, but in the lead-up: the missed details, the subtle shifts in behavior, the things that suddenly don't make sense. When written well, a mole creates dread in every quiet moment, every locked door, every glance over the shoulder.

Start by deciding **where the mole is buried**. Are they close to the protagonist—someone in their team, someone they trained, someone they love? Or are they higher up—a handler, a director, an ally in another department? The closer the mole is, the more emotionally devastating the betrayal becomes. Use ChatGPT to brainstorm levels of access: *"List five positions inside an intelligence agency where a mole could do maximum damage without being obvious."* Pick one and build them into your story's world early—long before the twist.

Then focus on the **why**. What motivates your mole? Money, ideology, blackmail, revenge, a disillusionment with the system they once served? The most chilling moles aren't villains twirling mustaches. They're idealists. Patriots who believe they're saving lives by leaking secrets. Or they're broken souls, abandoned by the agency they served, now selling access to survive. Give them real motivations and conflicting emotions. Make them human. Ask ChatGPT: *"Give me a character sketch of a double agent who believes they're doing the right thing."* That contradiction is what gives them weight.

Now build the **leaks**. How does the mole operate? Dead drops? Encrypted channels? Whispered exchanges at diplomatic events? Think slow-drip sabotage—missions that fail for no clear reason, intel that turns out to be bait, assets who are suddenly compromised. Let the protagonist start to suspect, not because of one smoking gun, but because of too many small inconsistencies.

And here's the trick: let the reader doubt, too. Introduce multiple characters who *could* be the mole. Seed suspicion. Use behavior, silence, misdirection. A team member who's always one step behind. A character who asks too many questions. An ally who vanishes during a mission. Then double back. Let the obvious suspect be clean, and the quiet one—the one who smiled, who seemed loyal—be the knife in the ribs.

Ask ChatGPT for help building suspicion patterns: *"What behavioral cues might reveal someone is hiding a dual allegiance?"* Let those cues appear in scenes, subtly. A character misremembering a past mission. A slip of terminology they shouldn't know. Let the protagonist notice these things—but not act on them. Not yet. Build the pressure.

The moment of **discovery** should hit like a shiv in the dark. It shouldn't be neat. It should be messy. Maybe the mole is caught red-handed, or maybe the protagonist has to set a trap—one final operation meant to draw them out. And maybe they don't want to believe it. Maybe they hesitate. And that hesitation costs something—an ally's life, a critical mission, the collapse of trust.

When the mole is revealed, the betrayal must *reframe everything*. That briefing two weeks ago? Now it's clear why they asked that question. That mission that failed in Act I? It wasn't bad intel—it was *sold*. That conversation the protagonist replayed in their mind, thinking something felt off? It *was* off. The mole's presence doesn't just matter—it reshapes the story backward.

You can let the confrontation be explosive or restrained. Maybe it's a shootout in a safehouse. Maybe it's a quiet conversation in an abandoned office. Maybe it's a stare exchanged across a room where neither of them can act—yet. Ask ChatGPT for options: *"Write a tense confrontation between a spy and their trusted partner who has just been revealed as a mole."* Use what it gives you as a starting point, then layer in your character's history, their guilt, their rage.

And then ask: what happens *after* the mole is exposed?

Does the protagonist trust anyone again? Do they become more like the thing they've been fighting? Do they realize the system allowed the mole to flourish in the first place? Maybe your protagonist has to cover it up to prevent greater fallout. Maybe they're ordered to forget it ever happened. Maybe they let the mole go—because killing them would mean admitting how close they'd let them get.

In the end, the mole is more than a twist. They're a mirror. They reflect everything the protagonist fears becoming—and sometimes everything they already are. That's what makes them powerful. That's what makes them unforgettable.

Torture, Truth, and the Limits of the Human Mind

Torture is one of the darkest tools in the espionage thriller's arsenal. It sits at the edge of morality, legality, and humanity—and that's precisely why it carries such narrative weight. When you introduce torture into your story, you're not just raising the stakes. You're shifting the genre's emotional and ethical gravity. It's no longer about gathering information or saving lives—it's about testing the boundaries of the human psyche. The victim's. The interrogator's. The reader's.

But if you're going to write it, you have to write it **responsibly**.

Torture in political and espionage thrillers isn't about gore or shock value. It's about *control.* It's psychological before it's physical. And it raises profound questions: How much pain can a person endure before they break? How reliable is a confession extracted under duress? Can a person ever be the same after inflicting—or surviving—it?

To write this well, you need to understand what **torture is really about**: the destruction of autonomy. The person being tortured isn't just in pain—they're being stripped of the right to hold back, to protect what they know, to choose silence. The interrogator isn't just demanding answers—they're trying to bend a human being into submission, to own their will. That imbalance is what makes these scenes so harrowing—and narratively rich.

Use ChatGPT to help you explore historical and psychological insights with a prompt like: *"Describe psychological tactics used in modern interrogations designed to break resistance without leaving marks."* This research allows you to write scenes that feel real but avoid cliché or exploitation.

One of the most important truths about torture—often overlooked in fiction—is that **pain doesn't always produce truth**. In fact, many victims will say *anything* to make the pain stop. They'll invent stories. Confirm false narratives. Repeat what they think the interrogator wants to hear. That's where the drama lives—not in the pain itself, but in the *ambiguity*. Is what's being said real? Or is it the final, desperate lie?

Your character—whether the torturer, the tortured, or the witness—should reflect this ambiguity. Let your protagonist doubt the intel they extract. Let them question whether they've just been manipulated. Let them wrestle with the fact that even if the information is good, the method used to get it may have shattered something vital—trust, humanity, their own soul.

If your protagonist is on the receiving end, go deep into the **mental breaking point**. Before the body fails, the mind begins to fracture. Sleep deprivation, isolation, sensory overload or deprivation, mock executions—these are the tools that unmake a person. Ask ChatGPT: *"List the long-term psychological effects of sensory deprivation on trained operatives."* Use the answers to craft a journey that's more than physical survival. Make it existential.

You don't need to write graphic detail. In fact, sometimes the most disturbing scenes are the quiet ones. The sterile room. The unseen scream. The cold voice asking questions the victim doesn't want to answer—not because they can't, but because they still believe they can hold on. Let the fear sit in the silence between questions. Let the reader imagine what's happening just off the page.

And don't forget the **interrogator's journey**. Torturers in fiction are often cardboard villains, but in a well-written thriller, they're something else. Maybe they believe in the cause. Maybe they're following orders. Maybe they've learned to disassociate, to see their victim as a threat—not a person. Or maybe they hate what they've become. Show the psychological toll. Show the rationalizations. Show the moments when the mask slips, and they realize they're losing their grip on morality.

You can even flip the dynamic. Maybe the torturer begins to question the mission. Maybe the victim gets inside their head. Maybe the act of inflicting pain starts to unravel the interrogator instead. Use ChatGPT to help you write these moments with internal conflict: *"Write an internal monologue of an interrogator realizing they're beginning to empathize with their subject."* These are the moments that linger—when the lines between right and wrong blur until there's nothing but regret.

Of course, not all torture looks like torture. There's **psychological warfare**: leveraging personal guilt, using threats against loved ones, replaying traumatic events. There's **chemical interrogation**—truth serums, psychoactive drugs. There's **manipulative interrogation**: friendliness, feigned sympathy, manufactured trust. Let your reader sit in the discomfort of these scenes. Let them feel the betrayal as much as the brutality.

And what happens after? That's where the real consequences lie. Your character might escape. They might survive. But they don't walk away clean. Flashbacks. Guilt. Aversion to touch. Loss of identity. Even the torturer may never sleep soundly again. Torture leaves **moral residue**—stains that don't wash off with victory. Ask ChatGPT to help build post-traumatic symptoms for either side. Use those scars to guide how your character acts in the chapters that follow.

In the end, writing about torture in a thriller isn't about glamorizing pain—it's about interrogating power. It's about showing the cost of information, the danger of control, and the fragile boundaries between hero and villain when desperation sets in.

Political Thrillers Set in the Corridors of Power

Some of the most chilling political thrillers never leave the comfort of air-conditioned offices, polished marble floors, and whispered conversations in wood-paneled rooms. There are no shootouts. No foot chases through foreign cities. But in the corridors of power—inside parliaments, intelligence headquarters, private boardrooms, and diplomatic chambers—the real battles are fought with information, influence, and carefully timed silence.

Writing thrillers set in these spaces is about harnessing tension from *stillness*. Every room holds secrets. Every character guards an agenda. Every handshake is a transaction. And every silence is loaded. The weapons aren't guns—they're policy memos, surveillance briefings, leverage files, and whispered threats that never get recorded. When done well, these stories unnerve the reader by revealing how much control exists behind the scenes—and how fragile that control really is.

To set your thriller inside the corridors of power, begin by crafting a **central institution**—one that holds real influence and is tangled in politics. Maybe it's a government agency. Maybe it's the executive branch of a crumbling democracy. Maybe it's a covert council of corporate and intelligence elites. You don't need a global conspiracy at first—just a system with cracks, rivalries, and unspoken rules. Ask ChatGPT to help define one: *"Create a fictional government agency that serves as a secret intelligence advisory body to the president."* This becomes your setting, your pressure cooker, your arena.

Characters in this world are **not soldiers—they're operators**. They don't need brute force. They have proximity to power, and they know how to use it. These are aides who bury files in procedural paperwork. Lobbyists who steer billion-dollar decisions with a single sentence. Generals who don't bark orders—they whisper recommendations into the right ear at the right time. And the most dangerous of all? The person who always seems *harmless*. The smiling assistant. The underestimated chief of staff. The one who's always in the room—but never speaks unless they have to.

Your protagonist can be a mole, a whistle-blower, a cynical insider, or even an idealist walking into this world and slowly realizing what it costs to play the game. They don't need to be hunted in alleyways. They just need to be watched. Shunned. Discredited. Or quietly removed. Use ChatGPT to develop a protagonist whose power is limited—but whose access is everything: *"Give me a character sketch for a junior intelligence analyst who discovers classified information that threatens national security."*

Conflict arises not from open opposition, but **from hidden agendas and layered truths**. Let the protagonist overhear one sentence that changes everything. Let them find a document that was never supposed to be seen. Let them realize a friend or mentor has been using them to pass information. The corridors of power are where betrayals are dressed in civility, and justice is often traded for stability.

And then there's the **architecture of fear**. In this world, power is protected by bureaucracy. Everyone is replaceable. The phone lines may be tapped. The elevators may have eyes. And one wrong move doesn't just end a career—it ruins reputations, silences witnesses, or quietly arranges a resignation letter that was never written by the person who signed it. Ask ChatGPT to help develop internal threats: *"Describe how a character might be slowly neutralized within a government agency without realizing it."* Let that slow unraveling bleed into the pacing of your scenes.

The tone of these stories is claustrophobic. You don't need to move locations constantly. You stay in the same rooms, the same floors, the same elevators—because *that's* where the real control is. Let the drama happen in hushed voices, double meanings, glances exchanged during press briefings, a footnote in a report that carries more danger than a bullet ever could.

This kind of thriller leans heavily on **dialogue and implication**. Characters rarely say what they mean. They deflect, hint, and provoke. Ask ChatGPT to help you write subtle conversations between rivals or allies: *"Write a tense exchange between two intelligence officials who both know a cover-up is underway but neither can speak openly."* These are the conversations where your thriller breathes—where every sentence tightens the grip.

And remember, these corridors aren't just about government. Power exists in corporate boardrooms. In think tanks. In media empires. In closed-door meetings between lobbyists and lawmakers. The corridors of power are wherever decisions are made by the few that shape the lives of the many. Your antagonist might be a government insider—or a foreign diplomat. A defense contractor. A CEO whose product fuels a silent war.

The climax of this kind of thriller isn't always an explosion. It's a vote. A press release. A carefully timed leak. A resignation that sends shockwaves through the system. Or maybe the climax is the moment when your protagonist walks away—exposed, ruined, but with the truth in their hands.

Political thrillers set in these spaces are powerful because they mirror reality. We know these places exist. We see their reflections in headlines, in scandals, in hearings and denials. And when you pull back the curtain in your story, the reader isn't shocked because it's unbelievable—they're unsettled because it *is* believable.

Writing the Intelligence Analyst as a Reluctant Hero

In a genre full of trained assassins, field agents with guns in their socks, and operatives who blend into foreign crowds like ghosts, the intelligence analyst can seem like an unlikely hero. But in the corridors of power, in the war rooms of policy, and in the quiet isolation of secure terminals, analysts are the ones who *see* what others don't. And sometimes, that's exactly what makes them dangerous.

The analyst is the one who pieces things together. Who notices the anomaly. Who spots the pattern others ignored. They're not supposed to be on the front lines—but sometimes the truth they uncover drags them there anyway. And that's when the real thriller begins. Writing the intelligence analyst as a reluctant hero gives your story a unique emotional dimension. They're not just fighting the enemy—they're fighting the system, their own fear, and a creeping realization that knowing too much can get you killed.

Start by defining what kind of analyst they are. Signals intelligence, cyber analysis, satellite interpretation, counterterrorism, political risk—they all offer different narrative tools. A satellite analyst might spot movement in a supposedly demilitarized zone. A cybersecurity expert might detect data leaks pointing to a mole. A counterintelligence analyst might find that a briefing has been doctored. Ask ChatGPT: *"Describe the daily responsibilities of a counterterrorism analyst inside a national intelligence agency."* Use that to build a credible world around your character.

The reluctant hero doesn't begin with a mission. They begin with a question. A puzzle. A pattern that won't sit right. They're not trying to be brave—they're trying to understand. And that's what makes their arc powerful. They're drawn into the crisis not by orders, but by *compulsion*. Something they see. Something they can't 'unsee'. Something no one else is taking seriously.

You can layer their initial reluctance in tone and behavior. Maybe they hate confrontation. Maybe they've seen how the agency devours whistle-blowers. Maybe they're burned out, jaded, or carrying guilt from a past failure. Whatever the reason, they don't want to be involved—but the threat becomes too big to ignore. Use ChatGPT to help flesh out the psychology: *"Give me a character profile of an emotionally repressed analyst who uncovers a threat but is afraid to report it."*

The beauty of this archetype is that they don't fight with fists—they fight with knowledge. Let their strength come from intellect, intuition, and the courage to speak up when everyone else stays quiet. Maybe they find a connection no one else did. Maybe they decode a transmission others dismissed. Maybe they challenge the official narrative—and that puts a target on their back.

What makes their journey compelling is how quickly **knowing something becomes dangerous**. The moment they raise a flag, things begin to shift. A hard drive is wiped. A supervisor suddenly questions their clearance. A meeting they were scheduled to attend is abruptly cancelled. Maybe someone tries to silence them outright—or worse, *discredit* them. Because in a world ruled by information, truth is the most volatile weapon of all.

This gives you the perfect setup for a **cat-and-mouse structure**. The analyst is out of their depth. They don't know how to evade surveillance. They're not trained to spot a tail. But they're smart. And desperation sharpens instincts. Maybe they turn to a former field agent for help. Maybe they go rogue and leak the intel. Or maybe they build their own network, using backchannel contacts and digital breadcrumbs to stay one step ahead.

Their reluctance gives way to resolve—but not heroism in the classic sense. Even when they act, they act from necessity. And the more they're forced to break rules to do what's right, the more blurred their moral compass becomes. They begin to ask the same questions field agents have lived with for years: *What's the price of the truth? Who am I serving? How far am I willing to go?*

The character arc is rooted in **transformation**. By the end of the story, the analyst may have become someone they barely recognize. They're harder, more suspicious, more aware of how power actually works. But they've also become bolder. And maybe—just maybe—they're ready to stop watching history unfold and start shaping it.

Ask ChatGPT to sketch that arc: *"Describe the transformation of a reluctant intelligence analyst who becomes a whistle-blower over the course of a political thriller."* These emotional pivots are the heart of your story. It's not just about stopping an attack or exposing a conspiracy—it's about who your character becomes on the way to doing it.

And that transformation doesn't always end with vindication. Maybe they're proven right—but no one cares. Maybe they're discredited. Maybe they disappear. Or maybe they're pulled deeper into the system and offered a promotion that ensures their silence. Let the ending be sharp. Let it sting a little. Because in political thrillers, the reward for doing the right thing often isn't applause. It's exile, loneliness, or a job offer they never wanted but can't afford to refuse.

The Lone Wolf: Writing Rogue Agents

In the world of political and espionage thrillers, few characters burn as brightly—or as unpredictably—as the rogue agent. The lone wolf is someone who knows the system from the inside but has decided to work outside it. They're dangerous not because they're unpredictable, but because they *know* exactly how the game is played—and choose to break the rules anyway. Whether they've gone rogue for revenge, redemption, justice, or pure survival, rogue agents make compelling protagonists, formidable antagonists, or both.

Writing a lone wolf is not about creating a one-man army with endless gadgets and a license to thrill. It's about writing a character who has **been betrayed**, or who has seen enough corruption to know that staying loyal would mean becoming complicit. They've reached a breaking point—and now they're operating without backup, without clearance, and often without mercy.

To write this archetype effectively, begin with the **fracture point**. What made your character walk away—or get cut off? Was it a botched mission that cost innocent lives? A superior who ordered something they couldn't morally justify? A realization that their agency is being used as a political weapon? Ask ChatGPT: *"Give me five plausible reasons why an elite intelligence operative might go rogue."* Choose the one that creates the deepest personal conflict.

Rogue agents are compelling because they live in a state of **constant contradiction**. They've been trained to serve a system they no longer trust. They still use the tools of their former life, but not the rules. They still have connections, but every one of those connections is a risk. They have no chain of command, no secure net to catch them. And every time they move, they risk being seen as the threat—by the very people they once protected.

This creates a **chase dynamic**—they are hunter and hunted. Maybe they're trying to stop a threat that their own agency refuses to acknowledge. Maybe they're being blamed for something they didn't do. Maybe they're chasing a former ally who went darker than they ever could. The tension isn't just in the action—it's in the *isolation*. Let them feel the silence after reaching for a contact who's too scared to answer. Let them walk through a safehouse they once trusted, now stripped and compromised. This is someone operating with nothing but instinct and unfinished business.

The lone wolf needs a **code**—something that keeps them from falling into pure vengeance or chaos. Maybe they won't harm innocents. Maybe they still protect the weak. Maybe they believe in the mission, just not the people running it. This code becomes more important the longer they stay in the shadows. It keeps the character grounded and gives readers a thread of morality to hold onto, even as the world around them fractures.

You can use ChatGPT to help define this internal compass: *"Describe a moral code for a rogue operative who still believes in justice but no longer trusts the government."* Let this code be tested repeatedly. That's where your story's emotional grit comes from—not just the shootouts and chases, but the moments where the rogue must choose between their old training and their new truth.

Writing the **psychological state** of a rogue agent is just as important as writing the external conflict. They might suffer from burnout, PTSD, paranoia. They might struggle to trust anyone. They might begin to wonder if they've become the very thing they were trying to stop. Let them question themselves. Let them spiral a bit. This isn't a superhero—they're human, raw, and on the edge. Ask ChatGPT for psychological traits: *"What are common behavioral patterns of long-term* *field operatives suffering from betrayal trauma?"* Build those traits into quiet scenes—alone in motel rooms, watching old news clips, scrolling through encrypted messages that never get replies.

A good rogue agent also forces the **institution to react**. Maybe the agency sends someone to kill them—or worse, to bring them in quietly, deny everything, and erase the problem. Maybe a younger agent is assigned to track them and begins to question the story they've been told. Maybe someone inside starts to sympathize and secretly feeds them intel. Let your rogue spark internal chaos in the system they left behind. They're not just a rogue. They're a *threat to the lie* that keeps everything running.

And then there's the question of **redemption vs. destruction**. Is your character trying to make amends, or just burn the whole thing down? Are they trying to stop something worse than themselves—or have they accepted that they're now part of the darkness? You can let ChatGPT help sketch endings: *"Describe three possible fates for a rogue agent in a political thriller who uncovers a global conspiracy."* Let the climax reflect the full cost of going off-grid—physically, emotionally, ethically.

You can also give them a foil. Maybe someone still inside the agency, someone who represents who they used to be—or who they could've become if they'd stayed. Let them confront each other in a way that brings ideology to the surface. These aren't just gunfights. They're philosophical debates, fought in looks, silences, confessions, and gun barrels trembling in the dark.

By the end of the story, the rogue agent may be dead. Or exiled. Or reluctantly welcomed back with conditions. Or maybe they disappear for good, becoming a rumor, a whispered name, a cautionary tale. The important thing is that their **actions changed something**. They forced a truth into the light. They made the system bleed. They gave someone else the courage to ask, *What am I really serving?*

When the Enemy Is Your Own Government

One of the most disturbing and potent storylines in any political or espionage thriller is the moment when the protagonist realizes the true enemy isn't across the border—it's across the hallway. It's not a foreign power, not a rogue actor or cyber cell in a hostile country. It's *home*. The agency. The administration. The government they swore to serve.

When the enemy is your own government, the thriller takes on a darker, more intimate tone. Loyalty becomes poison. Patriotism becomes a trap. And every move the protagonist makes is not just a fight for truth or justice—it's a fight for identity. Because what do you do when the system you dedicated your life to turns out to be corrupt, compromised, or complicit?

Start by defining what kind of betrayal your character uncovers. Is it a **systemic conspiracy**, like a secret surveillance program on citizens or the suppression of key intelligence to protect corporate allies? Is it **personal**, like being ordered to frame someone innocent? Or is it **ideological**, a slow realization that the system doesn't serve the people—it serves itself? Ask ChatGPT: *"Give me examples of morally gray government actions that could inspire a protagonist's crisis of conscience."* Use these to build the moment of awakening.

This shift must hit hard. The protagonist may have believed in their mission. They may have bled for the flag, worked late into the night building operations they thought protected lives. That belief is what makes the betrayal feel personal. They weren't just following orders—they believed they were on the right side. And now? Now they're expendable. Or worse—now they're the one being hunted.

Let the betrayal unfold **slowly at first**. A classified file that doesn't match the after-action report. A mission that goes sideways for no clear reason. A whistle-blower silenced and smeared. Then escalate. Someone close to the protagonist disappears. Surveillance footage is deleted. Their access gets quietly restricted. An old colleague tells them to stop asking questions—for their own safety. Let ChatGPT help pace this: *"Create a timeline of subtle warning signs that a government operative is being set up by their own agency."*

This isn't just paranoia—it's reality catching up. And when they finally realize the truth, they're forced to make a decision that changes everything: stay quiet and survive, or go loud and risk becoming a fugitive in their own country.

What makes this storyline powerful is the **emotional whiplash**. It's one thing to be betrayed. It's another to be betrayed by something you gave your life to. Let your character struggle. Let them want to believe the rot is isolated. Let them try to fix it from the inside—until they realize the system isn't broken. It's functioning *exactly* as it was designed to. That's the horror.

And now, they're up against a machine with unlimited resources. Intelligence networks. Surveillance tech. Media control. Legal tools. Friends turn cold. Phones go quiet. Safe-houses vanish. They don't just have to disappear physically—they have to disappear *digitally*, *legally*, *historically*. Let the story feel like a slow erasure of identity. They're not just escaping capture—they're escaping deletion.

This is where allies become vital—and dangerous. Maybe a rogue journalist agrees to help. Maybe a former handler feels guilty. Maybe a foreign government offers protection... at a price. Every hand extended could be a trap. Every leaked truth could be used as leverage. The character must navigate a world where trust is a currency that's rapidly depreciating.

Ask ChatGPT: *"Give me a list of ways a government might covertly neutralize a former operative who knows too much."* Use this to shape the threats. Psychological pressure. Financial strangulation. Manufactured criminal charges. A 'leak' that paints the protagonist as unstable. The machine doesn't need bullets to kill you—it can make the world stop believing you ever mattered.

But here's the key: this storyline doesn't work without a **moral center**. Your protagonist must believe in something. Maybe they believe the people deserve the truth. Maybe they're trying to protect someone who didn't sign up for this. Maybe they want redemption for the things they did before they realized what they were really serving. That belief is what drives them forward—when running, fighting, hiding, and surviving stop being enough.

And when it comes to **resolution**, you don't need a neat ending. Maybe they expose everything—but the story is buried. Maybe they release the files—but the public doesn't care. Or maybe they vanish into exile, always watching, always wondering when the next shadow will come for them. Let the ending reflect the weight of what's been uncovered. Let it sting. Because when the enemy is your own government, the real victory isn't survival—it's *refusing to become like them.*

This kind of thriller feels uncomfortably real because it plays with the oldest fear in modern democracy: that the institutions built to protect us might turn against us the moment we stop being useful. And that fear is what gives your story resonance, relevance, and power.

Exploring Themes of Surveillance and Control

In the world of political and espionage thrillers, surveillance isn't just a tool—it's a theme. A shadow. A warning. It's not just about who's watching—it's about *why*, and what happens to the people who know they're being watched. In stories where power is wielded quietly and control is more psychological than physical, surveillance becomes the invisible hand shaping lives, choices, truths—and even reality itself.

To explore surveillance and control as themes, you have to look beyond the spy cams and wiretaps. It's not the tech that matters—it's the effect. It's how people behave when they *know* they're being observed. How systems shape perception. How governments and corporations manipulate truth through constant monitoring. And most of all, it's how your characters begin to *change* once they realize freedom is a carefully constructed illusion.

Start by defining the **surveillance structure** in your story. Is it government-run? Corporate? A rogue system once designed for good that's now being repurposed? Use ChatGPT to help you craft the architecture: *"Design a modern surveillance program used by a fictional intelligence agency to track internal dissent."* Include facial recognition, social media scraping, biometric analysis, predictive algorithms. The more plausible it feels, the more unsettling it becomes.

Then let your protagonist encounter it. Maybe they're flagged for an anomaly in a report. Maybe their email gets rerouted. Maybe they notice the same car parked across the street three days in a row. Don't make it overt right away. Make it subtle. Creeping. Let the reader feel the paranoia building with every unreturned message, every locked door, every erased text.

Surveillance works best in fiction when it's **quiet and comprehensive**. Show your character hesitating before speaking near their phone. Let them change routes walking home. Let them start covering cameras with tape and turning off smart devices. These small changes in behavior reflect something bigger—*fear of being controlled through visibility.*

Now connect surveillance to the larger idea of **control**. What is the watcher trying to influence? Is it behavior, loyalty, ideology, or obedience? Maybe surveillance isn't about catching criminals—it's about *training citizens to stay silent*. It's not just a net—it's a fence. And your character, once inside it, starts seeing the invisible lines that shape every decision.

This creates fertile ground for exploring **resistance**. How do people fight back against something they can't see? How do you organize in a society where every word is recorded, every contact tracked, every browser click catalogued? Ask ChatGPT: *"List covert methods characters could use to communicate while under 24/7 surveillance."* The responses can inspire codes, dead drops, analog solutions, even personal relationships that exist entirely in silence.

Surveillance also becomes **internalized**. Your character may begin censoring their own thoughts, doubting their memory, rewriting their past. This is where control goes deepest—not through force, but through compliance. Not through violence, but through self-editing. That shift—from freedom to obedience—is what makes this theme so powerful.

You can mirror this through your antagonist. Maybe they believe the surveillance is necessary. Maybe they're former idealists who saw chaos and decided order mattered more than liberty. Maybe they believe knowledge is safety. Let them articulate their reasoning in eerie, rational terms. "If you have nothing to hide, you have nothing to fear." "We monitor to prevent harm." "It's not about control—it's about protection." That's what makes it so terrifying: it *almost* sounds reasonable.

Let ChatGPT help build philosophical conversations. Ask: *"Write a dialogue between a government surveillance director and a civilian whistleblower debating the ethics of total observation."* Use that exchange to reflect the ideological heart of your story.

The deeper your characters go, the more they'll realize **control isn't just watching people—it's *deciding what they see.*** Algorithms that feed them only one side of the truth. News stories that shift focus from scandal to spectacle. Search engines that erase histories. In this world, control is narrative, and surveillance is the editorial hand that shapes it.

And finally, consider the emotional toll. What does it do to someone to know they're never alone—not in their home, not in their thoughts, not in their memories? Maybe your character stops trusting themselves. Maybe they lash out. Maybe they break. Or maybe they go dark—off-grid, off-script, off the record. But even then, the fear lingers.

When you explore surveillance and control as themes, you're tapping into something deeply primal: the need to be free, the right to think privately, the desperate urge to *own your life*. These are not abstract concerns—they are immediate, intimate, and real. And that's why your thriller will resonate.

Whistle-blowers, Leaks, and the Price of Truth

In the world of political and espionage thrillers, few figures carry as much narrative gravity—or risk—as the whistle-blower. They're the ones who choose to speak when silence is safe. Who put their lives, careers, families, and freedom on the line to bring a hidden truth into the light. They aren't spies. They aren't soldiers. They're ordinary insiders who've seen too much—and decided they couldn't live with it.

But in these stories, truth isn't a cure. It's a weapon. And often, it's a wound.

Whistle-blowers and leakers walk the tightrope between heroism and treason. Some see them as patriots. Others, as traitors. That duality gives your thriller depth. It turns every revelation into a moral storm, where readers must decide for themselves if your character did the right thing—or simply created a bigger disaster in the name of principle.

Start by deciding **what your character exposes**. Is it a covert operation targeting civilians? An illegal surveillance program? A false-flag attack designed to justify war? The more believable it is, the more terrifying it becomes. Ask ChatGPT: *"List ten real-world inspired intelligence scandals that could be fictionalized in a thriller."* Choose one and reshape it. Don't just think about the leak—think about the system that would kill to keep it buried.

Your whistle-blower doesn't need to be a field agent. They can be a data analyst. A linguist. A janitor with a good memory and access to the wrong hallway. That's the unsettling power of this archetype: they're *not supposed* to be the one who brings down an empire. And yet, they do.

What matters most is the **reason they speak up**. No one leaks classified material lightly. Maybe they saw something they can't "unsee". Maybe they were part of it and can't sleep anymore. Maybe someone they love got caught in the crossfire. Or maybe it's just one line too far—and they decide enough is enough. Use ChatGPT to help sketch their motivation: *"Describe the emotional breaking point of a government employee who decides to leak a top-secret program."* Let that moment shape their entire arc.

Now build the tension. Leaking isn't immediate—it's a process. Gathering the evidence. Figuring out who to trust. Choosing between media, watchdog groups, or foreign intelligence agencies. Every step is laced with risk. Every message might be monitored. Every password might be a trap. Let the reader feel the weight of it.

And once the leak goes public—everything changes.

The government scrambles. Denials are issued. Counter-leaks discredit the whistle-blower. Old social media posts get twisted into smears. Family members are harassed. Bank accounts are frozen. This is where the thriller gains urgency—not from gunfire, but from **systematic erasure**. Your protagonist isn't just hunted. They're *disappeared* in real time.

Ask ChatGPT: *"How might a government discredit a whistle-blower without resorting to violence?"* You'll get ideas for character assassination, legal suppression, media manipulation, and institutional silence. Use those tactics to deepen the fear, and to show the true cost of telling the truth.

Your whistle-blower may go underground. Or they may go on trial. They may be forced to flee to another country. Or they may be locked in a room with a pen and a nondisclosure agreement. The aftermath of the leak is often more important than the leak itself—because that's when the moral questions hit hardest.

Did it change anything? Was it worth it?

Let the reader sit in that uncertainty. Maybe the public is outraged for a week—then moves on. Maybe the system adapts and tightens its grip. Or maybe the leak sparks global protests and fractures long-standing power structures. The outcome doesn't have to be tidy—but it must feel honest.

Whistle-blower characters also offer the perfect opportunity to explore **conflicted alliances**. Maybe a journalist helps at first—but backs off when it gets too hot. Maybe an old friend inside the agency warns them, then turns them in. Maybe someone who offered protection was a trap all along. These betrayals and half-betrayals mirror the central tension: *What is the price of truth?*

And don't be afraid to blur the lines. Maybe your whistle-blower isn't pure. Maybe they leaked for revenge. Or fame. Or to protect themselves. Maybe they only gave part of the story. Or maybe they didn't fully understand the consequences of what they revealed. Let readers question their motives—even as they root for their survival.

In these stories, truth doesn't set anyone free. It exposes. It isolates. It creates new enemies. But it also creates cracks in the wall. It plants doubt. It forces conversations. And sometimes, that's enough.

As you build your whistle-blower thriller, let the character's journey reflect that toll. Let them lose friends. Let them question themselves. Let them change—not into a hero, but into someone who knows what it means to hold a secret too long, and to finally let it go.

Constructing a Villain Who's a Political Powerbroker

In a political or espionage thriller, the most chilling villains don't hide in bunkers or stalk rooftops. They sit in the highest offices, walk the most secure corridors, and speak softly at press briefings while directing entire wars with a pen. A true political powerbroker villain doesn't need to pull a trigger. They just need to pull the right strings. Their strength lies not in force, but in influence—across governments, agencies, media, and minds.

These villains are rarely outwardly evil. They don't snarl or sneer. They're composed, well-spoken, often even charming. Their menace lies in what they can do *without raising their voice*. To write one well, you need to build a character whose power is systemic. Someone who understands that politics isn't about ideals—it's about *leverage*. And they always have it.

Start by choosing their **platform of power**. Are they an elected official? A senior intelligence figure? A defense contractor CEO with access to everything and accountability to no one? A diplomat with secret ties to multiple governments? Ask ChatGPT: *"List five high-level political roles that could serve as cover for a corrupt powerbroker in a political thriller."* Pick the one that gives your villain long reach and deep protection.

Now define their **motivation**. What do they *really* want? It's not always just control or wealth. Maybe they believe in stability over truth. Maybe they see democracy as a flawed system that needs managing from the shadows. Maybe they want to engineer a war to reset a global balance of power. Or maybe they started out trying to do good—and slowly redefined "good" to justify every compromise they made.

What makes them terrifying isn't just what they want. It's how *easily* they achieve it.

These villains rarely operate alone. They move through **networks**—advisors, lobbyists, private security firms, journalists, and compromised operatives. Their power is distributed. They don't dirty their hands because someone else will do it for them. Use ChatGPT to help design this infrastructure: *"Create a power structure around a corrupt Secretary of Defense, including insiders and silent allies."* This becomes your villain's shield and sword—able to act through others while keeping their own name clean.

And they're not always in opposition to your protagonist—*at first*. In fact, they might be the one offering help. Guidance. Resources. Maybe your protagonist works for them. Maybe they owe them a favor. Maybe they trust them. That makes the reveal all the more devastating when the protagonist finally sees what's really happening. This slow-burn betrayal adds depth and narrative weight.

Your political powerbroker should be a master of **language and timing**. They know what to say, when to say it, and—more importantly—*when to say nothing*. Let them manipulate not through threats, but through insinuation. Let them control through plausible deniability. Their words carry the weight of a thousand invisible consequences. Ask ChatGPT to help script: *"Write a scene where a politician threatens a whistle-blower without using direct language."* These scenes are where your villain's strength shines.

Then, give them **public virtue and private menace**. Let them be praised in headlines, awarded medals, spoken of as a patriot. Maybe they fund hospitals, launch peace talks, and pose for photos with children. But behind closed doors, they reroute black budgets, authorize blackmail, and sanction operations that silence dissent. This duality makes them feel real—and untouchable.

One of the most chilling aspects of this villain is that they're often *right*. Or at least, they sound like they are. They speak in cold logic. If a few people must be sacrificed to avoid a larger conflict, so be it. If a lie preserves national unity, then it's not really a lie—it's policy. They see themselves not as villains, but as *the grownups in the room*. Let readers feel the seductive pull of their reasoning. Let them wonder: if I had that power... would I do the same?

And don't make them invincible. Make them **adaptable**. When the protagonist strikes a blow, they pivot. When a leak threatens exposure, they spin it. When an ally betrays them, they already have a replacement. This doesn't mean they're untouchable—it means they're resilient. And it means your protagonist will have to be *smarter, bolder, and more ruthless* to take them down.

But taking them down can't be easy. Maybe the price of exposing them is too high. Maybe doing so creates a power vacuum that someone worse might fill. Or maybe your protagonist wins—but no one believes the truth. That ambiguity, that *cost*, is what makes the victory feel real.

Finally, consider their **legacy**. Even if they're defeated, what remains? Their systems? Their policies? Their influence? Maybe they're just one head of a hydra. Or maybe they've trained a protégé, just as cunning, waiting in the wings.

The political powerbroker villain is compelling because they mirror a fear so many people share—that real power isn't loud or obvious, but quiet, polite, institutional, and permanent. And that the world isn't shaped by heroes with guns—it's shaped by people who know where the bodies are buried, and who wrote the law that made burying them legal.

Making Dialogue Sharp, Secretive, and Suspicious

In political and espionage thrillers, words are weapons. Every line of dialogue carries weight, conceals intent, or lays the groundwork for betrayal. Characters rarely say what they mean. They speak in riddles, hint at truths, and use silence as punctuation. Conversations don't just move the plot forward—they *disguise* the plot, mislead the characters, and draw the reader deeper into the web of suspicion.

When dialogue is sharp, secretive, and suspicious, it elevates your thriller. It creates tension without action. Conflict without explosions. And suspicion without confirmation. You want your readers leaning closer, not because of what's said, but because of *what isn't.*

Start by understanding that in this genre, **dialogue is strategic**. Characters don't just talk—they calculate. Each line should serve an agenda. One character wants information. The other wants to deflect. One wants to test loyalty. The other wants to pretend everything's fine. The tension isn't in what's being said—it's in the *mismatch of intent*. Ask ChatGPT: *"Create a dialogue where one intelligence agent is trying to confirm if the other is a mole, without asking directly."* That prompt can give you the kind of slow-burning exchange that says everything without saying anything at all.

Keep your dialogue **tight and loaded**. Long speeches rarely belong in this genre unless they're masking a threat or revealing something a character *shouldn't* know. Use short sentences. Clipped answers. Pauses. Interruptions. These are the fingerprints of people who think before they speak—and who worry that saying too much might get them killed.

Also make use of **coded language and metaphor**. Your characters might speak about "weather patterns" when they mean political shifts. They might reference a chess game, a historical event, or a shared memory that contains the real message. This technique not only adds intrigue—it reinforces the genre's atmosphere of secrecy and paranoia.

Ask ChatGPT: *"Give me five examples of coded language spies might use in everyday conversation."* Use these to color your dialogue with layers of meaning.

Now add **subtext**. What a character *says* is only part of the story. What they really mean—that's where the thrill lives. A line like, "I heard you were in the building late last night," sounds innocent. But in context, it's a warning. Or an accusation. Or a confirmation that someone is being watched. Let readers feel the tension between words and intentions.

You can also build suspicion through **inconsistency**. Let a character's story change slightly. Let them react too quickly. Let them repeat phrases, deflect questions, or pretend not to know something they *definitely* should. Dialogue becomes suspicious not just because of content, but because of *context*. Ask ChatGPT: *"Write a conversation between two operatives where one begins to suspect the other is hiding something based on their answers."*

Characters in this world often lie. But the most effective lies are *partial truths*. Let a character reveal just enough to be credible—but hide the critical detail.

For example:

"We lost contact with the informant after Berlin."

"And no one followed up?"

"We were told not to."

That last line shifts the mood. Who gave the order? Why? Suddenly, a routine status report becomes something more. Every thriller thrives on these conversational cracks.

Tone and rhythm matter too. If a character normally speaks with confidence, a sudden stammer or change in cadence signals fear or dishonesty. If someone answers too quickly, or avoids a question with a joke or a story, that's your cue to dig deeper. Use body language to mirror the dialogue: a glance to the side, a hand that fidgets, a step backward after a direct question. These micro-tells give your scenes texture.

Suspicious dialogue is also a great tool for **misdirection**. Maybe two characters talk about an event in a way that misleads the reader. Maybe they're using the conversation to draw attention *away* from what's really happening. Let your readers figure it out one sentence at a time. Let them experience the uncertainty your characters feel. That's how you build trust in the story while creating doubt in every word.

And remember the power of **silence**. Sometimes, a character says nothing—and that's the most damning response of all. A pause that lasts too long. A question that gets ignored. A stare across the table that speaks louder than any line of dialogue. These silences are as important as speech in building mood, suspicion, and power dynamics.

To sharpen your dialogue:

- Rewrite until every line *needs* to be there.
- Cut anything that's on-the-nose.
- Ask what your character is really trying to say.
- Use interruption, evasion, or misdirection to build tension.
- Let emotion leak through restraint—not exposition.

Ask ChatGPT to help you polish: *"Tighten this exchange between a spy and their former handler who may be setting them up."* Then tweak the wording so each sentence is doing triple duty: plot, character, and threat.

In this genre, every conversation is a chess match. Every word is a piece. Every pause is a move. And every scene should end with someone realizing they're either a step ahead—or already cornered.

Layering in Romance, Lust, or Loyalty under Pressure

In political and espionage thrillers, romance doesn't exist in a vacuum. It's not leisurely, soft, or purely sentimental. It's complicated, loaded, and usually laced with suspicion. The stakes are high, the timing is terrible, and the pressure of looming betrayal or disaster makes every glance, every touch, every moment between characters feel more electric—and more dangerous. Whether you're layering in romance, lust, or loyalty, the key is to make these dynamics feel like *tension*, not a detour from it.

Romance in this genre is never just about love. It's about vulnerability in a world that punishes it. Lust is never just desire—it's distraction, leverage, risk. Loyalty isn't just about who you care about—it's about who you'll *betray everyone else for*. These emotional undercurrents raise the stakes in every scene, especially when the characters themselves aren't sure if their connection is real or tactical—or both.

Start with **proximity under stress**. Two people on the run. Two agents forced to share information—or hide it. A bodyguard and their high-value target. A handler and an asset. These relationships thrive in secrecy, confined spaces, and moments where death is a real possibility. That intensity accelerates closeness, but also amplifies doubt. Is it chemistry, or is one of them manipulating the other? Let the reader sit in that uncertainty.

Use ChatGPT to build scenarios that force closeness: *"Describe a situation where a field operative and their source must hide in close quarters during a lockdown, leading to romantic tension."* These situations can play out as emotional mines. Maybe they connect, maybe they nearly kiss, maybe they don't trust themselves to cross that line—because once they do, it changes everything.

Lust, in this genre, is often adrenaline-driven. It's impulsive, urgent, and never without consequence. A kiss at the wrong time. A night together that leads to a compromised operation. A moment of weakness exploited by someone who has their own agenda. Use it to show character conflict—because in thrillers, lust is rarely clean. It often comes with guilt, confusion, or immediate regret. And that's what makes it powerful.

Ask ChatGPT for variations: *"Give me five ways a spy might use seduction as a weapon, only to genuinely fall for their mark."* This gives you the duality you want: the line between performance and emotion. That's where the real tension lives—when your character isn't sure if what they're feeling is real, or just expertly played back at them.

Romance, when sincere, gives your protagonist something to lose. It softens them, but it also puts them in danger. If they fall in love, they're now vulnerable. The enemy can exploit it. The agency can use it against them. Let this connection force your protagonist to hesitate, to question orders, to risk everything. Let it make them unpredictable. Let it make them *human*.

But avoid melodrama. In a thriller, emotional beats should be *tight*, not indulgent. A single look across a room. A moment where one character patches up the other after a mission. A quiet conversation at 3 a.m., where someone admits they're afraid—not of dying, but of what they're becoming. Let the intimacy grow from necessity, not convenience.

Loyalty, too, must be tested. Especially when your characters are on opposite sides—or think they are. Maybe one is undercover. Maybe one has orders to betray the other. Maybe one of them already *has*. These moments crack open everything. Let loyalty be personal and professional at once. Let your characters be forced to choose: the mission, or the person who knows the truth about them.

A character who stays loyal under pressure becomes a point of stability. A character who *appears* loyal, but isn't, becomes a knife in the back. And a character who flips loyalties at the worst possible time? That's your twist.

Dialogue here becomes especially sharp. Characters don't declare their love—they imply it. They show it through defiance, through quiet protection, through hesitation when pulling the trigger. Let ChatGPT help you write those moments: *"Write a scene where a spy warns their lover with a coded phrase during a public meeting."* These subtle layers are more compelling than any dramatic confession.

And remember, romance and loyalty in thrillers aren't just subplot—they're *motivation*. The need to protect someone. The grief of someone lost. The betrayal of someone trusted. These emotional drivers move your story forward with just as much power as secrets and bullets.

As you write these relationships, keep asking: What happens if the trust breaks? What if one is using the other? What if they're both being used?

Because in espionage, even love can be weaponized.

Using Flashbacks to Reveal the Spy's Origins

In political and espionage thrillers, the spy is often a mystery—not just to the people around them, but to the reader as well. They're trained to compartmentalize, to hide what they feel, to erase their past. But somewhere behind the perfect cover, the stone-faced silence, and the loyalty to something bigger than themselves, there's a human being. Someone who started somewhere. Someone who became this.

And that's where flashbacks become one of the most powerful tools in your arsenal.

Flashbacks allow you to reveal the spy's *true self*, layer by layer. You're not just showing where they came from—you're building emotional resonance. You're explaining the moral lines they walk today by revisiting the ones they crossed long ago. You're giving context to their silence, their fear, their loyalty, their rage.

But flashbacks in thrillers must be used with precision. You can't stop the plot cold. You have to integrate them into the rhythm of the narrative, so they hit like echoes—resonant, haunting, and necessary. When done well, they don't slow the story down. They give it *depth*.

Start by defining **what the flashback reveals**. Is it the spy's first mission? A betrayal that shaped them? The moment they were recruited? The personal loss that still defines them? The lie they told that haunts them? Ask ChatGPT: *"List ten possible formative events in a spy's life that would make compelling flashbacks in a political thriller."* Pick one that ties directly to your character's current emotional state.

Your flashbacks should be **triggered by something tangible**—a face, a phrase, a file, a setting. Maybe a hallway reminds them of the training compound. Maybe a voice sounds like someone they left behind. Maybe a smell, a scar, or a sniper's perch takes them back to the moment it all changed. These triggers ground the memory in the present and make it feel natural rather than inserted.

Flashbacks are also a great opportunity to show **the spy before the spy**. Let the reader meet the person they used to be—idealistic, scared, angry, brilliant, or naive. That contrast adds emotional weight to everything they do now. A character who once promised never to kill, now making life-or-death decisions? That sticks. A character who trusted everyone, now refusing to say more than they have to? That's a transformation the reader *feels*.

Use ChatGPT to help write these before-and-after moments: *"Write a scene of a young intelligence recruit being initiated into black operations, followed by their present-day reflection on that moment."* These dual scenes can frame your chapters, echo one another, and pull tension between past and present.

Flashbacks are also where you can explore **themes of indoctrination, identity loss, and transformation**. Maybe your character didn't choose this life—they were shaped by someone else's agenda. A handler. A mentor. A government that promised purpose but delivered obedience. Let the flashback reveal not just *what happened*, but *how it was framed* at the time. And let the reader see the cracks forming.

Keep the flashback **visually distinct** in your writing. Change tone, style, even sentence rhythm if needed. Maybe the flashbacks are written in present tense. Maybe they focus more on sensory detail, because memory is tactile. Maybe they're colder, more distant—because the character has emotionally disconnected from that past. These shifts help the reader immediately recognize that time has changed.

Also consider using flashbacks to introduce **secondary characters** who no longer exist in the present—but whose impact still shapes the protagonist. A sibling. A lover. A former teammate. Someone the spy failed, saved, or betrayed. Their presence in the past can cast a long shadow over the present, especially if the spy sees someone who reminds them of what they lost.

Let ChatGPT help you craft those lost bonds: *"Create a backstory for a spy whose closest friend was left behind during a mission and is presumed dead."* Use that backstory to fuel the decisions they make now. Maybe they hesitate to leave anyone behind. Maybe they don't trust new alliances. Or maybe they're still looking for redemption.

Don't overuse flashbacks. Too many, and you'll deflate the tension. But strategically placed, they can deepen suspense, explain motives, and give the reader a chance to breathe—while also tightening the emotional noose.

The most powerful flashbacks often come **right before or after a moral choice**. Let your spy relive the moment they lost someone right before deciding whether to kill a target. Let them remember their first lie right after swearing they'd never lie again. Flashbacks are mirrors—and the reflection should challenge the choices being made now.

And finally, flashbacks are a reminder that in espionage, the most dangerous secrets are never the ones in files or databases.

They're the ones buried in memory.

The Hero's Journey with a Burn Bag and a Gun

The hero's journey in a political or espionage thriller doesn't involve magic swords or ancient prophecies. It involves encrypted laptops, forged passports, and a burn bag full of everything they can't afford to leave behind. This is a journey not of myth and destiny, but of survival, deception, and moral erosion. And yet, at its core, it follows the same timeless structure—a reluctant hero, a call to adventure, a fall from grace, and a final, irreversible transformation.

But this journey smells like gun oil and paper ash. And the dragon at the end might be wearing a three-piece suit.

When writing the hero's journey in this genre, you're dealing with a protagonist who starts the story deeply embedded in a system they believe in—or at least tolerate. They're a loyal agent, a quiet analyst, a field operative trying to finish one more mission. But something changes. They uncover a truth. A betrayal. A body that shouldn't be there. A lie that's too big to ignore. And in that moment, the journey begins.

The **call to adventure** often arrives as classified intel or a message intercepted by mistake. Maybe it's a routine surveillance file that doesn't add up. Maybe someone from the past shows up with a warning. Maybe the protagonist is ordered to carry out an operation that doesn't feel right. It's not a literal call—it's an *internal pull.* A suspicion. A tremor of conscience. A moment when they stop being part of the system and start questioning it.

At first, there's **refusal**. Because in the spy world, asking questions is dangerous. The hero might try to stay silent, bury what they found, or report it through "proper channels." That almost always makes things worse. The moment they break protocol—even a little—they're marked. They've crossed an invisible line, and now there's no going back. This is the burn bag moment: grab what you can, destroy the rest, disappear.

Now the **journey through the underworld** begins. The protagonist goes off the grid. They leave behind their identity, their support systems, their security clearance. They may become a fugitive. A traitor. A problem to be handled quietly. This is where the story shifts from duty to desperation. They're surviving on instincts, favors, and half-truths. And they're learning fast who they really are.

Ask ChatGPT: *"Outline a modern spy's version of the hero's journey where the agency becomes the antagonist."* Use it to map the beats of your protagonist's arc—from obedient functionary to rogue agent to reluctant revolutionary.

Along the way, your hero meets **allies and enemies**—some clearly defined, some morally grey. A cynical journalist. A whistleblower in hiding. A former handler who's half-protector, half-threat. A love interest who may be bait. These characters test the hero's values and push them toward transformation. Every conversation is loaded. Every meeting could be a setup. But the hero keeps going because what they've uncovered is too big, too dangerous, and too close to ignore.

The **ordeal**, or midpoint of the journey, is usually a major confrontation—an ambush, a betrayal, or a truth bomb that shatters the last shred of faith the hero has in the system. Maybe they discover their mentor is dirty. Maybe they learn that they were part of a lie all along. Maybe they're forced to do something they swore they'd never do. This is the moment that breaks them. It's not always physical. Sometimes it's emotional. Psychological. Existential.

But in that breaking comes the **rebirth**. The hero begins to operate on their own terms. They don't trust the flag anymore—they trust their gut. They're no longer running. They're moving forward with purpose. Maybe it's revenge.

Maybe it's justice. Maybe it's simply stopping something before it escalates. But now they're not just reacting. They're *acting*. And the system that trained them no longer owns them.

This leads to the **climax**—the final confrontation. It might be a leak. An assassination. A showdown in a data center or a closed-door hearing. It's the moment when the truth comes to light—or is buried again, but not without consequence. And it's the moment when the hero must decide who they really are: the tool, the traitor, or the torchbearer.

The **return** doesn't always come with a parade. In fact, it rarely does. Maybe the protagonist is exiled, hunted, erased. Maybe they survive in a cabin with a new identity and nightmares. Or maybe they're back in the system, but with eyes wide open, playing a different game. What matters is that they've changed—and they've forced the world around them to change as well.

And that's the heart of the spy's hero's journey. Not to defeat evil outright, but to *survive truthfully* in a world built on lies. Not to save the world, but to stop it from collapsing in on itself. Not to kill the dragon, but to show the people who feeds it.

This version of the hero's journey is sharper. Colder. Built from ashes, not fire. But it follows the same emotional current: from ignorance to understanding, from obedience to independence, from silence to voice.

And when your protagonist zips up the burn bag and tucks the gun into their belt, they're not becoming a hero in the traditional sense.

They're becoming someone the system should have never underestimated.

When the Entire World's a Lie: Writing Paranoia

Paranoia is not a subplot in a political or espionage thriller—it's a *state of being*. It's the air your characters breathe. The lens through which they see every face, every file, every conversation. In a world built on secrets, where loyalty is currency and truth is just another manipulated variable, paranoia isn't madness. It's *survival instinct*.

Writing paranoia well means immersing the reader in that constant dread. It's not about sudden scares or jumpy behavior—it's about the slow erosion of certainty. The gradual collapse of what the character thought they could trust. The terrifying realization that even the people closest to them might be part of the illusion.

Start with your protagonist's **perception shift**. At the beginning of the story, they might be cynical, but functional. They follow protocol, trust their clearance level, respect their chain of command. But something happens—a mission that goes wrong for the wrong reason, an inconsistency in a report, an order that doesn't feel right. It doesn't need to be explosive. It just needs to be *wrong enough* to make them start asking questions.

That's the spark. The paranoia doesn't come all at once. It *builds*.

Ask ChatGPT: *"Give me a sequence of escalating events that would cause a spy to begin questioning their own agency's intentions."* Use those steps to guide your pacing. Let the character find a name where it shouldn't be. A file edited without explanation. A contact who no longer exists. And let every piece of new evidence *undermine something familiar*—an old friendship, a mentor's story, a personal memory.

Paranoia intensifies when the protagonist starts to question not just the system, but **themselves**. Did they remember the meeting wrong? Did they misread the order? Did they fabricate the threat because they wanted something to be wrong? Use internal dialogue to reflect this confusion, but keep it grounded. Your reader should be just as unsure as the character.

This is where **unreliable narration** can become a powerful tool. Not necessarily because your protagonist is lying, but because they don't know anymore what's real. They start to notice every camera. Every glance. Every hesitation in someone's voice. They begin to decode *everything*—and maybe they're right. Or maybe they're spiralling. You don't have to answer that outright. Let the reader squirm in that gray space.

You can ask ChatGPT: *"Write a scene in which a government agent receives a friendly message that seems threatening only because they're unraveling emotionally."* Use this to play with tone and implication. Make the innocuous feel loaded. That's the essence of good paranoia.

Create moments where **the mundane becomes sinister**. A phone that rings once and stops. A briefcase that's slightly out of place. A recurring face in a crowd. Let these details accumulate. Separately, they're nothing. Together, they become a pattern—and in thrillers, *patterns mean danger*.

Paranoia becomes especially gripping when it threatens relationships. Let your protagonist begin to doubt the people they love. Maybe their partner is asking too many questions. Maybe their handler is "checking in" more often than usual. Maybe a trusted colleague deflects when pressed. Whether these suspicions are valid or not is almost beside the point—because paranoia *isolates*. It turns every ally into a potential enemy. And it forces the protagonist to carry the weight of the truth *alone*.

Don't forget the **physical toll**. Sleep deprivation. Stress-induced illness. Constant surveillance (or the belief in it). Let your character begin to crack. They forget passwords. They start rehearsing conversations before they happen. They imagine what they'd say under interrogation. Not because they've been compromised—but because they *expect to be.*

Use ChatGPT to sketch these changes: *"Describe the mental and physical effects of long-term surveillance and professional betrayal on a covert operative."* These details help your character feel real—and make their unraveling all the more gripping.

Paranoia doesn't always lead to clarity. Sometimes the big reveal never comes. Sometimes the conspiracy *wasn't there*—but something else was. A personal betrayal. A subtle manipulation. A long game played by someone who was always two steps ahead. Or maybe the paranoia *was* justified—but too late to stop what's coming. That ambiguity is essential. It mirrors how paranoia feels: desperate, disorienting, and rooted in *almost-truths.*

Dialogue in paranoid thrillers should reflect this tension. Characters rarely say what they mean. Their words feel like veiled threats, their compliments like tests. One character might say, "You're doing good work," but the protagonist hears: *They're watching me.* These layers of meaning are what keep readers on edge.

And remember: in a paranoid world, even *silence* is dangerous.

Let your setting reflect the atmosphere. Fluorescent lights that hum too loud. Offices that always feel too quiet. Windows that look out onto empty courtyards. Let your thriller feel like a surveillance tape on loop—too perfect, too still, too intentional.

Finally, let your protagonist change. Paranoia isn't a temporary mindset—it becomes a *new way of seeing.* Whether they're proven right or left with questions, they'll never be the same. They won't trust doors, names, or faces the way they used to. They'll walk into the light wondering what's behind them.

Because once you know the world *might* be a lie—you can never quite believe in it again.

The Countdown: Adding Time Pressure to Your Plot

In political and espionage thrillers, nothing tightens the tension quite like a ticking clock. A deadline—real or perceived—strips away hesitation, pushes characters to their limits, and forces decisions that reveal who they truly are. Whether it's 48 hours to stop an assassination, 12 minutes before a data file auto-deletes, or seven days before a government collapses, time pressure transforms your story from a slow-burn mystery into a breathless race against fate.

But time pressure isn't just about pacing—it's about **urgency**. It's the crackling energy behind every scene, the tightening vice on your protagonist's psyche, and the enemy that never sleeps. When done right, it keeps readers glued to the page not because they want to know what happens, but because they feel like they *have to know now*.

To use a countdown effectively, you first need to establish the **stakes**. What happens if the clock runs out? A virus spreads. A traitor escapes. A file goes public. A city burns. The tighter the consequences, the higher the tension. Ask ChatGPT: *"List high-stakes scenarios for political thrillers that could unfold under a 24-hour countdown."* Choose one and build everything around it.

Then choose your **unit of time**. Some thrillers use hours or days. Others use seconds. You can even stretch time across an entire book—counting down to a key event like an election, a vote, or the signing of a peace accord. The trick is to start the countdown at a moment when the protagonist is *least ready to act*. This gives the story a frantic undercurrent and ensures every decision is a gamble.

The countdown works best when it's **embedded in the story world**, not just tacked on. A phone alert. A mission briefing. A surveillance feed with a live timer. A code that expires. A bomb with a red LED blinking in the dark. Let the characters see the clock ticking. Let the reader *feel* the seconds slipping away.

Time pressure also lets you **compress structure**. Everything becomes faster. Tighter. Characters speak in fragments. Tension spikes. Information is scarce, mistakes are costly, and hesitation gets people killed. Ask ChatGPT: *"How would a covert operation shift if the time window for success shrank from five hours to thirty minutes?"* This kind of question helps you reshape entire plot beats to reflect that pressure.

The beauty of a countdown is that it **intensifies character conflict**. If you had weeks, you might build a team. Double-check facts. But with hours? You rely on the wrong person. You act on incomplete intel. You tell the truth too late—or not at all. Time becomes the scalpel that cuts into loyalty, love, and logic. The reader watches characters fray at the edges because they don't have the luxury to hold it together.

Use this pressure to **strip away pretence**. Maybe the protagonist starts by following the rules. But as the deadline nears, they start breaking them. They go off-book. Lie to their superiors. Cut off allies to move faster. The closer the clock gets to zero, the more we see who they really are. Let ChatGPT help you explore this evolution: *"Describe the moral unraveling of a spy under increasing time pressure to complete a high-stakes mission."*

And don't forget to give your **antagonist a clock too**. Maybe they're trying to beat the same deadline. Maybe they're setting it. Or maybe they're using the countdown to manipulate the hero—leaking information to burn time, sending false leads, or faking a deadline to trigger a bad decision. The time pressure becomes a weapon wielded by both sides.

The countdown can also structure your story visually. Open chapters with timestamps. Use time markers in scene headers. Show clocks on screens or in dialogue: "We've got nine hours." "The vote's in five minutes." These references give your story a constant pulse—and keep readers aware of every second lost.

And sometimes, the **deadline moves**. Maybe the team thinks they have three days—only to learn they have six hours. That shift causes panic. Desperation. You can also fake out the audience. Maybe the clock hits zero—and nothing happens. It was a distraction. Or the *real* threat activates then. These twists make time not just a background element, but a dynamic force in the plot.

Finally, pay off the countdown with **impact**. If the hero fails, make it matter. If they succeed, show what it cost. Don't let the climax arrive without blood, loss, or consequence. The countdown exists to push everyone past their limits—and the resolution should feel like the final gasp after a breath held too long.

Because in a world of lies, pressure, and power, the clock is the one thing that doesn't negotiate.

Real World Locations That Enhance the Thrill

Setting matters in any thriller, but in a political or espionage story, it's not just backdrop—it's leverage. The right location doesn't just paint a pretty picture. It multiplies the stakes. It restricts choices. It reveals power structures, social hierarchies, surveillance culture, and the fragility of order. A government building can feel like a fortress. A crowded market can become a trap. An embassy might be a safe haven—or a cage. The world your characters move through should always be whispering the same message: *you're being watched, you're not safe, and time is running out.*

What makes a real-world location thrilling isn't the postcard beauty—it's the **friction between what it appears to be and what's really going on.** The romantic cafés of Vienna? Perfect cover for an intelligence handoff. A sunny square in Istanbul? Hiding an informant's execution under layers of everyday noise. The sterile calm of a Tokyo government facility? A mask for backdoor surveillance networks.

To use real-world locations well, you need to look at three things: **symbolism**, **functionality**, and **layers**.

Start with **symbolism.** Your locations should resonate with the themes of your story. If your spy is questioning the cost of obedience, place them in Berlin—where walls were torn down, but the scars of division remain. If your thriller explores global corruption, set scenes in Geneva or Brussels, where international diplomacy masks corporate manipulation. Ask ChatGPT: *"List global cities that represent secrecy, diplomacy, or political tension for use in a spy thriller."* Use this to align place with meaning.

Next is **functionality**. Every location should serve the plot. Not just as a place where something happens—but as a reason why it *has* to happen there. The protagonist meets their handler in a London Underground tunnel because GPS fails there. The leak occurs in a Seoul karaoke bar because the noise masks the drop. The operative is cornered in a Nairobi hotel because it's a diplomatic neutral zone with no backup allowed. Let the architecture, law, and culture of the place directly impact the choices your characters make.

Then come the **layers.** Great locations in thrillers are never just one thing. A French vineyard is also the entrance to a Cold War-era listening post. A rooftop in Mumbai is a sniper perch and a surveillance blind spot. A private school in Cairo is both a recruitment ground and a communications hub. These layers give your scenes depth and mystery. Ask ChatGPT: *"Describe hidden intelligence infrastructure in real-world public spaces."* You'll find places readers recognize—now infused with threat.

Here are a few **notable real-world locations** that enhance the thrill:

- **The Kremlin (Moscow)**: A seat of power, dense with history, paranoia, and secrets. Any scene here instantly feels high-stakes.
- **Langley (CIA Headquarters, USA)**: Quiet, clinical, and impenetrable—until it isn't.
- **Checkpoint Charlie (Berlin)**: A symbol of betrayal and blurred lines. Great for ghosts of the past resurfacing in the present.
- **The DMZ (Korea)**: Still technically at war. Ideal for stand-offs, prisoner exchanges, or dangerous diplomacy.
- **GCHQ (Cheltenham, UK)**: Less flashy than the CIA, but crawling with data, codebreaking, and watchers watching the watchers.
- **The UN General Assembly (New York)**: A place where everyone's listening and no one's telling the truth.

- **The Pantheon (Rome)**: Historic, sacred, and packed with tourists—perfect for a public meeting with private consequences.
- **The BND Headquarters (Berlin)**: Sleek, modern, cold—and known for being extremely secure. A heist here is audacious.
- **Hong Kong's Mid-Levels Escalators**: Constant movement, close quarters, perfect for tailing someone without being seen.
- **The tunnels beneath Paris**: Not just catacombs—old escape routes, hidden cells, long-forgotten war bunkers.

These are not just places—they're **pressure points**. They come with built-in tension. Political histories. Laws that complicate pursuit or protection. Local customs that hide danger in plain sight. Choose locations that challenge your characters, that restrict their usual tactics, or that evoke emotional memory they can't afford to face.

Don't over-describe. Focus on **sensory specifics** that signal danger: the echo of footsteps in a marble hallway, the flicker of a camera in an embassy ceiling, the faint scent of smoke in a supposedly empty room. Let the environment be a silent character—observing, influencing, exposing.

And use **contrast**. The more ordinary a location feels, the more shocking it is when violence or betrayal erupts. A seaside resort where a diplomat's family vacations—until a courier dies in the pool. A crowded subway car where a secret changes hands beneath oblivious passengers. These juxtapositions make the tension sing.

Finally, always let the location do more than decorate. Let it *trap*, *expose*, *echo*, or *hide* something. Let it reflect what your protagonist is going through—lost in the maze of their own past while navigating Prague's winding alleys. Or boxed into a moral corner in a stark D.C. conference room with bulletproof glass and too many witnesses.

Because in a great political thriller, setting isn't just setting.

It's a weapon.

Using ChatGPT to Flesh out Subplots and Supporting Characters

In a political or espionage thriller, the main plotline—the leak, the mission, the betrayal—often moves at breakneck speed. But the world surrounding that plot, filled with subplots and supporting characters, gives the story depth, realism, and texture. Without them, your thriller might be tense but hollow. With them, it becomes layered, immersive, and unforgettable.

Subplots and secondary characters serve one crucial purpose: **they make the story feel like it's bigger than the protagonist**. A great thriller doesn't revolve around a lone hero solving everything—it unfolds across multiple perspectives, where even the smallest players influence the outcome in unexpected ways.

This is where ChatGPT becomes an invaluable creative partner. Used effectively, it can help you brainstorm, expand, and refine the web of relationships, motivations, and parallel conflicts that turn your thriller into a fully realized world.

Start by thinking about the **subplots that naturally emerge from your main plot**. Is there a journalist chasing a different angle on the same story? A junior agent assigned to monitor your protagonist who begins to sympathize with them? A family member back home who thinks everything is normal? These threads add layers of tension and give your protagonist's actions ripple effects.

Use prompts like:

"What are five subplots that could unfold alongside a political thriller about a rogue intelligence operative?"

"Give me ideas for a supporting character whose actions unintentionally compromise a covert operation."

"Create a subplot involving a diplomatic spouse who begins to suspect something is wrong."

These suggestions will help you build *organic side arcs* that connect thematically to your main story while giving you room to explore other tones—romantic, tragic, ironic, or redemptive.

Supporting characters are where your thriller gains its emotional gravity. They're more than foils—they're potential betrayers, confidants, red herrings, or martyrs. Use ChatGPT to design them with specific roles and emotional weight.

Try prompts like:

"Give me a character sketch of a disillusioned cyber analyst who might leak information."

"Describe a morally conflicted ambassador who is forced to choose between their country and their conscience."

"Write a backstory for a street-level informant who holds a secret they don't realize is valuable."

Don't just stop at their bios. Explore their voices, behaviors, and motivations. Ask ChatGPT to write sample dialogue:

"Write a tense conversation between a junior diplomat and their CIA contact in which neither wants to reveal what they know."

This is how you find the *texture*—the pauses, the lies, the misunderstandings—that make these characters feel alive.

You can also use ChatGPT to **track emotional arcs and transformations**. Maybe a bodyguard begins the story completely loyal, but slowly questions the morality of the person they're protecting. Maybe a mole starts to believe in the person they're supposed to sabotage. These arcs don't need to dominate the story—but they enrich it. And by the end, they create a sense that the entire world has changed, not just your protagonist.

Ask:

"Track a 5-beat emotional arc for a supporting character who starts as an antagonist but sacrifices themselves in the third act."

Another powerful use of ChatGPT is generating **interpersonal conflicts that aren't tied directly to the mission**. Maybe your protagonist's loyalty to a partner interferes with their orders. Maybe a character is secretly dealing with grief, addiction, or a moral debt they haven't paid. These subplots humanize your cast and create tension in scenes that don't require gunfire.

Use prompts like:

"What personal struggles could a seasoned intelligence operative face while trying to complete a mission?"

"Give me examples of emotional baggage a character might carry from a botched operation in the past."

You can also ask ChatGPT to show how two subplots can **collide or cross paths**:

"Describe how a subplot involving a whistle-blower journalist could accidentally reveal the location of an undercover agent."

This kind of creative cross-wiring keeps the tension high and ensures your story feels cohesive, not episodic.

And finally, don't forget that **some supporting characters exist only to test your protagonist**. The character who challenges their worldview. The one who offers a path out. The one who sacrifices themselves at the wrong time. Ask ChatGPT to help build these characters as *mirrors* and *triggers*.

Try:

"Create a character who represents the life the protagonist could have had if they walked away from espionage."

"Write a confrontation where a former friend accuses the protagonist of becoming everything they once hated."

These scenes become your emotional anchors—the parts your readers remember not just for the action, but for the feeling.

In sum, subplots and secondary characters aren't distractions—they're how you build the world *around* the mission. They make the lie feel deeper, the betrayal sting harder, and the truth feel more dangerous. And with ChatGPT's help, you can shape an intricate network of arcs, threads, and tensions that will make your story richer than ever.

Creating Cultural and Political Tensions with ChatGPT's Input

One of the defining features of a gripping political or espionage thriller is its ability to reflect, reinterpret, or distort real-world cultural and political tensions. These tensions don't just add realism—they deepen the conflict, raise the stakes, and give every decision a sense of historical and ideological weight. Whether it's a stalled peace process, a nationalist uprising, a cold diplomatic war, or the clash of global tech superpowers, the world your characters move through should feel tense, unpredictable, and uncomfortably familiar.

Creating those tensions authentically takes research and nuance—and that's where ChatGPT becomes a powerful tool.

Start with **real-world geopolitical flashpoints**. You don't have to copy them directly into your story, but you can use them as models or inspiration. Ask ChatGPT to help you identify active areas of conflict or strategic importance. For example:

"List current global hotspots where espionage or political manipulation could plausibly take place in a thriller."

You'll get locations like the South China Sea, the Korean Peninsula, Eastern Europe, West Africa, and cyberwarfare zones involving the U.S., Russia, and China. From there, you can create fictional nations or build a parallel reality inspired by these tensions. A good thriller doesn't need to mirror the world exactly—it just needs to *feel like it could.*

You can also ask ChatGPT to **simulate historical tensions** that mirror modern conflicts. Try:

"Summarize the political factors behind the Cold War arms race and how they could inform a modern cyberwar thriller."

"Describe how colonial legacies in Africa might impact current diplomatic relationships in a fictional thriller plot."

Now that you've anchored the geopolitical context, you can move into creating **cultural dynamics**. Culture influences everything—how your characters speak, trust, challenge authority, conduct operations, and interpret events. A misstep in etiquette could cost someone their life. A religious holiday could shield or disrupt a mission. A cultural taboo could become the key to understanding someone's hidden motive.

Ask ChatGPT to help build these layers:

"What are common cultural misunderstandings that could occur between a Western intelligence agent and a Middle Eastern informant?"

"List cultural dynamics in Japan that could affect how a political scandal is handled publicly and privately."

These responses can add texture and tension to even mundane scenes—like a meeting in a café, a handshake at a summit, or a dinner invitation with diplomatic strings attached.

You can also explore **character identity through political context**. Let ChatGPT assist with questions like:

"Create a backstory for a former Eastern Bloc agent still shaped by Cold War ideology, now working for a private cyber-intelligence firm."

"Describe a young activist turned reluctant informant, caught between loyalty to their cause and pressure from a Western intelligence agency."

These character sketches allow you to show how personal and political beliefs collide—and how espionage exploits those cracks.

Now think about **institutional tensions**. Rival intelligence agencies. Politicians with opposing agendas. A diplomatic envoy sabotaging a peace process for private gain. Ask ChatGPT:

"Describe how inter-agency conflict between intelligence organizations might unfold during a joint operation in a volatile region."

"Give me examples of how multinational cooperation can be undermined by differing interpretations of a shared intelligence report."

These scenarios create not just external conflict, but **internal friction**, which is just as deadly. In a high-stakes thriller, the most dangerous enemy might not be on the other side of the world—it might be the person across the conference table.

Political thrillers also benefit from exploring **propaganda, public perception, and media manipulation**. You can simulate headlines, press briefings, or state-sponsored disinformation with a few precise prompts:

"Write two conflicting news headlines from different countries covering the same espionage incident."

"Create a leaked memo from a fictional intelligence agency spinning a failed operation as a success."

This kind of material isn't just world-building—it becomes plot fuel. What the world *thinks* is happening can be even more powerful than what's really going on.

To further develop cultural and political complexity, try writing scenes from **multiple national or ideological perspectives**. Ask ChatGPT to take on roles:

"Write a conversation between a Chinese diplomat and an American journalist discussing a cyberattack on a global bank."

"Create a tense negotiation between a South American revolutionary leader and a UN mediator trying to secure a ceasefire."

These types of scenes help you explore not just what characters want, but *why they see the world the way they do*. And that's where real tension lives—not in who has the gun, but in who thinks they're *right*.

Even seemingly small elements—like **translation errors**, **symbolic gestures**, or **protocol violations**—can become catalysts for conflict.

Ask ChatGPT for ideas:

"List diplomatic mistakes that could trigger international scandal at a peace summit."

Use those missteps to trigger your plot's unraveling or to reveal the friction under polished surfaces.

Finally, use these cultural and political tensions to ask **bigger questions** through your story. Does stability matter more than truth? Can peace be bought? Is nationalism always dangerous—or just when weaponized? Let ChatGPT help you explore these ideas through dialogue, setting, and backstory—not to give answers, but to ask them more sharply.

Because in a great political thriller, the most thrilling thing isn't the car chase or the coded message.

It's the *realization* that people believe their actions—no matter how destructive—are justified by history, culture, and necessity.

Writing Action Scenes That Read Like Tactical Ops

In a political or espionage thriller, action scenes shouldn't feel like generic Hollywood brawls or aimless gunfights. They should feel surgical. Controlled. Specific. When a covert operation goes loud, the action should still feel like an extension of the training, objectives, and calculated risks that define real-world espionage. Tactical action isn't about spectacle—it's about **intention, precision**, and **what happens in the silence between each movement.**

Writing action that reads like a tactical op means more than just describing gunfire and movement. It's about immersing the reader inside the mind of someone trained to assess risk in microseconds, to read shadows as threats, to understand the architecture of a room as a battlefield. Every bullet counts. Every movement has a purpose. And every mistake could collapse the mission—or expose the truth.

Start with **objectives**, not violence. In real tactical operations, every action has a goal: secure a target, extract an asset, disable surveillance, intercept a courier, or neutralize a threat without collateral. Use this to structure the scene. Don't just drop your character into a firefight—drop them into a **mission**. Ask ChatGPT:

"Outline the steps in a black-ops mission to extract a hostage from a foreign safehouse under heavy surveillance."

That outline becomes the spine of your action. Each movement and shot should drive the mission forward—or highlight how the mission is starting to fail.

Before you write the sequence, **map the environment**. Know the layout of the location: the entry points, exits, vantage spots, camera coverage, potential chokeholds. Use ChatGPT to generate detailed locations with spatial logic:

"Describe the interior layout of an embassy's restricted wing during a high-security protocol shutdown."

This lets you choreograph the action like a chess match, not a brawl. The more grounded the space, the more visceral the scene becomes.

Now build the **team dynamic**. If your operative is working solo, what tools are they using—thermal optics, silenced weapons, 'comms' jammers, breaching gear? If they're working with a team, assign roles: point man, rear guard, demo specialist, sniper. Let their communication reflect training: short, clipped, coded language.

Ask ChatGPT for realism:

"Write radio dialogue between four operatives during a silent breach of a compound."

This helps you find the rhythm of a real tactical team—disciplined, synchronized, and focused under fire.

Tactical action thrives on **timing and pressure**. The first shot isn't fired casually—it's a pivot point. The breach isn't noisy unless it has to be. Delays increase the danger. Decisions made in seconds could result in injuries, blown cover, or international scandal. Let the protagonist make those decisions fast—and make the consequences hit hard. You want the reader to feel the split-second cost of every move.

In these scenes, **every sensory detail matters**, but not in purple prose. You don't need to describe the sunlight on the floor—you need to describe how that light blows their concealment. Focus on the operationally significant: the weight of the suppressed pistol, the sweat inside a Kevlar vest, the smell of cordite and antiseptic in a medical safe-house. Ask ChatGPT:

"List sensory details an operative would notice during a night-time assault on a government facility."

Use those details not to beautify, but to **weaponize tension**. Let each one suggest danger, exposure, or shifting control.

Keep **language short and deliberate**. Long sentences slow action. Tactical writing is clipped, like the thinking of the operative under fire. But make sure your reader always knows **where they are**, **what's happening**, and **what the stakes are**. Chaos is part of action—but confusion is not.

Also consider **perspective**. A third-person limited view can heighten tension by locking readers into the operative's field of knowledge. They don't know what's around the corner. They're guessing. Adapting. Listening to footfall on tile and counting how many breaths are in the next room. That's what makes the scene immersive.

Let ChatGPT help draft or tighten these scenes:

"Write a 300-word tactical action scene from the POV of an operative clearing a floor in a dark office building after an alarm has been tripped."

Then layer in *obstacles*:

- Communications jammed.
- Target not where expected.
- Friendly fire potential.
- Unexpected civilian presence.
- Weapons malfunctioning.
  These complications force your characters to adapt under fire—and that's where you separate soldiers from survivors.

And don't forget: the **fallout matters**. A true tactical op scene isn't about "cool action." It's about the *results*. Who's injured. What was lost. What was discovered—or covered up. Let your characters regroup. Let them debrief. Let them feel the adrenaline crash, the guilt, the panic about what went wrong or what's coming next.

You can even use ChatGPT to simulate these moments:

"Write a post-operation debrief between a team leader and a handler where one key agent is missing."

That scene may say more about the mission—and the emotional stakes—than the firefight ever could.

Finally, remember that great tactical writing isn't just about realism. It's about *emotional precision*. The audience should feel the cost of every breath, every gunshot, every decision your character makes under pressure.

Hacking, Tracking, and the Digital Battlefield

In today's political and espionage thrillers, the battlefield isn't just physical—it's digital. Conflict plays out in invisible layers of code, signals, and data. War isn't declared—it's leaked. Power isn't taken—it's hacked. And intelligence isn't just gathered in dark alleys—it's scraped from smartphones, satellites, servers, and social feeds. Writing compelling scenes on the digital front means understanding how technology shapes the game—and how your characters fight battles they can't see with weapons they can't touch.

This is where thrillers become *modern*—when laptops become more dangerous than rifles, and data leaks are more explosive than bombs.

Start by understanding that the **digital battlefield is asymmetric**. One person in a basement can breach a billion-dollar system. An outdated security patch can topple a government. Your protagonist doesn't need an army—just a connection, a toolset, and a goal. And your antagonist doesn't need a weapon—they just need access. ChatGPT can help you explore these dynamics with prompts like:

"List five cyberattack strategies that could destabilize a national security operation in a political thriller."

From there, anchor your conflict in one or more of the three core domains: **hacking, tracking, and exposure**.

Hacking is the most iconic and cinematic. But writing it well means *avoiding the Hollywood clichés*. No walls of green code, no furious typing montages with countdown timers. Real hacking is quiet. Patient. Specific. And most of all, **purpose-driven**. Your characters don't hack systems because they can—they hack for leverage, for access, for silence.

Use ChatGPT to design realistic intrusion points:

"Describe how a covert agent might breach a secure government email server using a compromised Wi-Fi printer."

"Outline a phishing attack that tricks a defense contractor into downloading malware."

Make the process feel believable. Your hacker might create a spoofed website, clone login credentials, install a remote access trojan, or escalate privileges inside a network. These details don't need to be technical for the reader—they just need to feel authentic and *consequential*.

Tracking is the spy-craft of the digital age. Your characters can be traced through GPS, cell towers, smart devices, browser histories, facial recognition databases, biometric ID systems, and more. But the real thrill comes from turning that around. Maybe your protagonist plants a location beacon in a rival's vehicle. Maybe they erase themselves from a traffic cam network. Maybe they follow a digital breadcrumb left behind by someone who tried to disappear.

Ask ChatGPT:

"Give me five ways an intelligence agency might track someone in a modern city without direct contact."

Or:

"Describe how a spy could go completely dark—digitally invisible—for 72 hours."

This allows you to build both tension and strategy. Maybe your character is being hunted through every device they've ever touched. Maybe they're ghosting a surveillance net that was designed for people exactly like them.

Exposure is where your digital thriller becomes political. Leaks. Metadata. Dossiers. Social engineering. False information seeded online. A single encrypted drive could contain names that topple a presidency. A manipulated video could start a war. The character who controls the flow of *information* often holds more power than the one holding the gun.

Use ChatGPT to simulate this digital chess match:

"Write a scene where a hacker threatens to leak classified intel unless their demands are met—but the recipient suspects the data is a bluff."

These are the moments where stakes become psychological, political, and personal. Because in the digital age, reputation is as vulnerable as infrastructure.

You can also build tension using **timed exploits**—the equivalent of a bomb with a countdown. A virus that will activate unless a file is deleted. A set of stolen emails set to auto-publish if the protagonist is compromised. A GPS tracker embedded in a loved one's smartwatch. Let the reader feel the clock ticking through signal strength, blinking icons, or the words "connection lost."

Don't forget the **environment**—the setting of your digital battlefield. A coffee shop with open Wi-Fi where a hacker spoofs a server on the next table. A locked server room in a corporate skyscraper. A midnight code drop in a data center. The world of wires and waves is physical, too. Let your characters break in, jack in, and get out—fast.

Use ChatGPT to generate these environments:

"Describe a secure facility that stores digital intelligence on foreign assets in cold storage."

"List common weaknesses in modern building security that a cyber-infiltrator might exploit."

Character dynamics also play out differently in digital conflicts. Your protagonist might never meet their enemy face to face. They may know them only by handle, by code signature, by digital fingerprints. Or maybe they realize too late that their enemy *is inside the system they trust*. A government firewall. A mobile app. A voice assistant in their apartment.

Paranoia blooms fast here. Ask ChatGPT:

"How might a digital surveillance AI hide its presence while observing a covert agent?"

Let that sense of omnipresent observation creep into your character's mind. A camera that lingers too long. A text message that echoes a private thought. A locked file that opens after years—and changes everything.

And finally, make sure the digital plotline **connects emotionally**. It's not about bytes—it's about betrayal. A character realizes they were tracked through their child's device. A mission fails because a smartwatch pinged in the wrong place. A trusted analyst turned traitor by logging one file too many. These moments aren't tech—they're *personal violations*.

Let the code become character. Let the system feel alive. And let the battlefield be everywhere—because in a digital war, there are no borders.

Spies, Satellites, and Signals Intelligence

If human intelligence (HUMINT) is about whispers, glances, and back-alley exchanges, then signals intelligence (SIGINT) is about patterns, transmissions, and data that never lies—until someone tells it to. In modern political and espionage thrillers, the most powerful spies aren't just carrying guns or sneaking through borders. They're decoding encrypted messages, intercepting global phone calls, and watching entire nations from thousands of miles above Earth.

When you add satellites and SIGINT into your story, you're writing on a **global scale**. Your characters aren't just slipping through embassy gates—they're navigating a world of invisible information streams, tracking targets through airwave footprints, and piecing together intelligence from fragments of intercepted chatter.

Let's start with **what signals intelligence actually is**. It's the interception, processing, and analysis of electronic signals—from military radio traffic and diplomatic emails to cellular metadata and radar emissions. It's how nations spy without stepping foot on foreign soil. And when you write it into a thriller, it adds an eerie omniscience to the story. Someone *somewhere* is always listening.

Use ChatGPT to get a foundational understanding fast:

"Explain how SIGINT works in an intelligence operation, including real-time and archival interception."

From there, think about **what's being collected**. It might be real-time surveillance—like intercepting a satellite phone call between a general and an arms dealer. Or it might be deep storage—like combing through three years of encrypted traffic to find the one message that links a diplomat to a covert op.

In a thriller, SIGINT raises the stakes by suggesting *there is no such thing as private communication anymore*. Your protagonist might be on the run—but their phone pings a cell tower. Their email pings a server. Their face is tagged by a passing drone. SIGINT gives the enemy a reach that feels inescapable.

And then there are **satellites**—those cold, silent watchers in low Earth orbit. They're not just floating hunks of metal. They're eyes, ears, and memory. Some capture high-resolution optical images. Others detect infrared signatures. Some collect signals across entire continents. When your story brings satellites into play, the sense of scope becomes immense. Characters can't hide in crowds or deserts—they have to think *under radar*, behind thermal shielding, off the grid entirely.

Ask ChatGPT:

"List capabilities of modern surveillance satellites used by intelligence agencies."

Or:

"Describe a scenario where a satellite captures evidence of an international conspiracy."

These tools can do more than spy—they can confirm or disprove entire narratives. A character claims they were in Paris during an attack? Satellite footage shows their car entering Moscow. An airstrike is blamed on one nation, but infrared data proves the plane came from another direction. These are **plot-redefining moments**, made possible by invisible intelligence.

But SIGINT and satellite surveillance are also double-edged swords. They can *overwhelm* a story with abstraction unless you bring the data to life. Let your protagonist be the one decoding the chatter, isolating the pattern, spotting the anomaly. Give them access to a secure listening station in Alaska, a GCHQ analyst in Cheltenham, or a field laptop built for signal triangulation. The tools matter—but the **interpretation** is where the drama lives.

Maybe they find a rogue frequency being used by an unknown asset. Maybe they realize a friendly embassy is leaking intel through a corrupted relay. Maybe they trace a kill order back to someone inside their own government—because the metadata never lies.

Ask ChatGPT to create these twists:

"Give me a scenario where intercepted communication accidentally reveals a traitor inside the protagonist's agency."

SIGINT is also great for **planting misdirection**. Maybe the data stream is manipulated. Maybe the adversary uses deception tactics—false pings, fake files, digital noise. A clean signal doesn't always mean a clean truth. Let your characters wrestle with what they're seeing and what it *means*. Because in this space, *certainty is a liability*.

You can also use SIGINT to fuel **conflict between characters**. A field agent believes their source. An analyst insists the signal data proves otherwise. One wants to act on instinct. The other wants to follow the data. These internal clashes echo the bigger theme of modern espionage: *the tension between human intuition and machine-collected truth.*

Want to add intensity? Use real-time tracking. The target is moving. The signal is fading. The window to strike is shrinking. A team is in the field waiting for coordinates—but a storm is disrupting satellite feed. Let ChatGPT help:

"Write a high-stakes scene in which a surveillance team loses satellite contact during a live operation."

These moments inject urgency into the otherwise quiet, analytical world of signals intelligence. They force fast decisions based on incomplete data—exactly the kind of tension thrillers thrive on.

And finally, SIGINT and satellite technology allow you to explore **philosophical territory** too. Who watches the watchers? What happens when machines know more than their operators? When intelligence is gathered by faceless tech instead of flawed humans, where do we place responsibility?

Let your characters wrestle with these questions. Let a veteran spy distrust a satellite's evidence. Let an analyst question whether their surveillance is protecting freedom—or choking it. Let a political operative use signal manipulation to rewrite the truth in real time. These aren't just tech tools. They're *ethical dilemmas with antennas*.

Ending with Impact: Final Confrontations and Moral Cost

A political or espionage thriller isn't remembered for how it starts. It's remembered for how it *ends*. The final confrontation is not just about stopping the villain, exposing the plot, or escaping the last trap—it's about *revealing the cost*. Because no one walks away clean. Not in this genre. Not in a world built on secrets, betrayal, and hard choices made in the dark.

To end with impact, your story needs a confrontation that does more than close the plot. It needs to echo *everything your protagonist has been through*. The lies they've told. The loyalties they've burned. The truth they've uncovered. The truth they've buried. Your ending must ask the ultimate question: *was it worth it?*

Let's start with the **structure of the final confrontation**. This is the moment when your character and their adversary—be it a powerbroker, a former ally, a system, or an ideology—collide. The tension here should be less about whether they'll survive and more about what *they're willing to become to win*. This isn't always a shootout. Often, it's a conversation. A leak. A final choice that alters the course of everything that came before.

Ask ChatGPT:

"Write a climactic confrontation between a whistle-blower and a corrupt intelligence chief where both sides reveal personal compromises."

This will give you a layered dialogue, rich with subtext, confession, and the raw exchange of belief versus consequence.

The best endings in this genre force your character into a **no-win scenario**. They can publish the truth—but risk national collapse. They can assassinate the traitor—but lose their soul. They can walk away—but the problem persists. These choices resonate because they reflect the real-world ambiguity we recognize: in espionage, there is rarely a neat moral line. There is only *what you can live with*.

Consider using ChatGPT to test multiple versions of your final beat:

"Describe three different outcomes for a political thriller's climax where the hero must choose between exposure and survival."

Then ask: which ending leaves the reader not satisfied, but **haunted**?

Your climax should also revisit the **thematic threads** you've been weaving throughout. If your story has explored surveillance, then the final confrontation might play out through a live broadcast. If your theme is loyalty versus truth, then the character's final decision might be whether to protect someone they care about or let the truth destroy them. If paranoia has driven your plot, maybe the antagonist was never who they seemed—and the real enemy was behind the curtain the whole time.

Let the world react, but not too completely. The resolution can't be perfect. The fallout must feel **earned and unresolved**, because the genre reflects reality, not fantasy. A successful leak might go ignored. A mission might succeed, but only after costing an ally's life. The villain might fall—but their legacy remains intact.

You can ask ChatGPT to help build these shades of gray:

"Write an epilogue where the protagonist succeeds in their mission but is forced into exile to preserve global stability."

The **moral cost** of the final act is what makes it stick. Let your protagonist carry it. Maybe they live, but they're never the same. Maybe they go free—but someone else takes the fall. Maybe they bury the truth themselves—because they've learned that some truths destroy more than they save. These are the scars that stay with the reader.

The final scene of your book doesn't need to be loud. It needs to *echo*. A silent room. A character watching the news, knowing what *really* happened. A text message that reads: *It's done.* A drive handed to a stranger with the words, *"Don't lose this."*

Keep it sharp. Keep it subtle. Let the reader feel the weight.

And consider using a final line that *challenges the story* itself. A line that makes the reader go back, rethink, wonder. A quiet question. A private confession. A final lie.

Because the best espionage endings don't promise justice or peace. They promise that truth always has a cost. And someone—maybe the hero, maybe the villain, maybe the reader—has to pay it.

Cleaning Up Loose Ends without Killing the Suspense

A satisfying political or espionage thriller doesn't end with every plot thread tied in a bow—it ends with the right threads tied, the dangerous ones fraying, and a few hanging just long enough to make the reader uneasy. Cleaning up loose ends is essential to reward the reader's attention and effort—but do it too thoroughly, and you drain the tension. Do it too quickly, and you shortchange the emotional weight of the journey. The key is to leave just enough open to suggest the truth always runs deeper than we're allowed to see.

Your goal at this stage is *balance*. Readers want payoff, not perfection. They want resolution, not sanitization. They want to *feel* like the protagonist accomplished something, but also sense that the cost was real, and that the world your story lives in remains fundamentally unstable. Because in the thriller genre, especially one steeped in politics, espionage, betrayal, and lies, **too much clarity can feel false**.

So how do you clean up the mess without ruining the mystery?

Start by asking: **Which loose ends matter to the emotional core of the story?** These must be resolved. If your protagonist made a promise, broke a code, or betrayed someone, the consequences of those choices should be reflected in the final chapters. If a character vanished or switched sides, the reader needs closure—or at least the sense that someone is still *looking for the truth*. Ask ChatGPT:

"List five character-driven plot threads that should be addressed by the end of a political thriller to create emotional resolution."

Address them in ways that feel natural. A quiet visit to a grave. A phone call that's never answered. A letter slid under a hotel door. These are not big, showy resolutions—they're weighty silences.

For **plot-based loose ends**, you have more flexibility. Not every question needs an answer. In fact, *not answering* can be more powerful than over-explaining. If a leaked file vanishes, maybe it's because someone erased it. Or maybe it was never real. If a character is revealed to have a hidden past, you can leave it hinted at without detailing it. These unresolved elements keep the story alive in the reader's mind after they close the book.

Ask ChatGPT for ambiguity tools:

"Give me examples of ways to imply a conspiracy's survival without stating it directly."

Another technique is **subtle looping**—returning to a small moment or object from earlier in the book that now has new meaning. Maybe a briefcase the protagonist ignored holds a clue they now understand. Maybe a line of dialogue, once throwaway, now carries weight. These small echoes tie the narrative together without closing it off. They reward attentive readers without over-explaining.

Your **secondary characters** are often where unresolved tension can linger. A former ally who walks away without a word. A journalist still chasing something. A former asset still out there. These characters can act as shadows of the larger story—evidence that the game never really ends, just shifts players. Use their exits carefully. They don't all need big moments. Sometimes, a character simply disappears. That absence becomes the suspense.

Ask ChatGPT to help with small exits that leave big questions:

"Write a final scene where a secondary character disappears without explanation, but leaves behind a disturbing clue."

Then there's the **institutional fallout**. In a political thriller, exposing the villain doesn't necessarily fix the system. Maybe the agency disbands—but a new one forms. Maybe a scandal breaks—but another story buries it. Maybe the public never hears the truth. These elements maintain the genre's signature tension: *you can win, but you can't fix everything.* Let ChatGPT simulate realism here:

"Describe how a government might quietly absorb the consequences of a major intelligence failure."

Your protagonist doesn't need to solve every problem. They just need to *make a decision*—one that reflects who they've become and what they've learned. Whether they walk into the light, vanish into the shadows, or simply go home and live with it, *how* they end matters more than how much gets explained.

You can also use **visual metaphors** and subtle cues in the final pages to suggest what's left open. An encrypted file the protagonist chooses not to open. A name written in a notebook. A glance in a crowd. A drone hovering just a little too long. These become your dangling threads—ones that say, *there's still more story if you know where to look.*

And finally, use the **last line** to linger. It doesn't have to be dramatic. It just has to carry weight. A quiet realization. A recontextualized truth. A question that won't go away.

Something like:

"He deleted the file. But the backup still sat in her inbox, unread, waiting."

Or

"They told him it was over. That was the lie that scared him the most."

Editing Your Thriller in Hours, Not Weeks, with AI Help

Writing a political or espionage thriller is a high-wire act—plot threads everywhere, characters with layered motives, pacing that whips from silence to shootouts. By the time you reach "The End," you've likely rewritten scenes mid-draft, changed character arcs on the fly, and added last-minute twists that altered everything. What you're left with is a fast-moving, emotionally taut story that *feels* done... but isn't clean yet.

Now comes the part writers dread: **editing**. But with AI—specifically tools like ChatGPT—you don't need to spend weeks combing through every page alone. You can **streamline the process, sharpen your story's edge, and get your manuscript production-ready in hours**. It's not about letting AI do it all—it's about using AI to *accelerate and elevate* your creative decisions.

Here's how.

Start with the **big-picture structural pass**. Before you tweak sentences or search for typos, you need to make sure the story's foundation is solid. Give ChatGPT a brief overview of your plot and ask:

"Does this thriller's plot have a clear midpoint twist, escalating stakes, and a satisfying third act?"

This gives you a high-level diagnostic. If something feels rushed or flat, AI can help you identify weak links. Maybe the midpoint needs a stronger reversal. Maybe the final confrontation lacks emotional resolution. These insights save you from polishing scenes that may need to be restructured entirely.

Next, focus on **character arcs**. Feed ChatGPT brief summaries of your main characters—especially your protagonist and antagonist—and prompt:

"Does this protagonist have a clear internal arc from loyal agent to disillusioned whistle-blower?"

"Is the antagonist's motive believable, and does their ideology conflict with the hero's in a meaningful way?"

Let the AI flag inconsistencies or missed opportunities for thematic contrast or emotional payoff. If your spy loses everything by the end, did the beginning set up what that loss *meant*? If the villain is revealed to be right about something, was that foreshadowed?

Now jump into **scene-by-scene tightening**. You don't have to feed entire chapters—just summaries or snippets will do. Focus on scenes that feel off in pacing, tone, or clarity. Ask:

"Revise this scene to increase tension without adding length."

"Make this character's dialogue more clipped, like a veteran intelligence officer under pressure."

ChatGPT can clean up clunky phrasing, flatten exposition, or suggest stronger entries and exits for each scene—all while retaining your voice and pacing.

Then, focus on **line editing for tone and texture**. A political thriller thrives on restraint. The language should be sharp, deliberate, and weighted with subtext. Run a page or paragraph through the AI and ask:

"Make this description tighter and more suspenseful, like a passage from John le Carré or Jason Matthews."

The AI can help you remove redundant phrases, replace generic verbs, and rephrase action or introspection to sound cooler, smarter, and more spy-savvy.

You can even use AI to **balance exposition and action**. Thrillers often swing from info-dumps to explosive scenes—and finding the right rhythm between the two is key. Paste a chunk of exposition and ask:

"Rewrite this background information as subtle dialogue between two agents in a tense situation."

Suddenly, your intel dump becomes part of a layered exchange, maintaining flow and mystery while slipping the reader the facts.

Let's talk about **continuity and logic**—two major blind spots when you're close to the work. Ask ChatGPT:

"Does this sequence of events make logical sense within the constraints of government surveillance systems?"

"Did I maintain consistency in the portrayal of the mole from chapter 12 to chapter 29?"

This is where AI's memory and pattern recognition excel. You'll catch inconsistencies in names, timing, motivations, or tech usage—before your beta readers do.

Then, do a **final polish for clarity and speed**. Run small paragraphs or chapter summaries and prompt:

"Tighten this scene without losing its meaning. Aim for fast pacing and clean sentence flow."

A thriller must breathe fast. Paragraphs should glide, not drag. This edit gets your prose closer to cinematic.

Finally, use AI to prep for **agent or reader submission**. Create your pitch, logline, and blurb with help from prompts like:

"Write a 150-word synopsis of this political thriller that highlights its central conflict, main character, and unique hook."

This kind of framing helps you zoom out from the manuscript and see what kind of story you've really told. It also helps you understand what readers will latch onto—whether that's the character's emotional arc, the geopolitical intrigue, or the morally gray theme.

Editing with ChatGPT doesn't mean giving up control—it means working with a tireless, fast-thinking assistant who lets you focus on the decisions only *you* can make: the mood, the message, the moments that matter.

And in a genre where timing is everything, being able to edit your thriller in hours—not weeks—might just be your most tactical advantage yet.

Formatting, Final Polish, and Getting Ready to Publish

You've written the last chapter. The final twist landed, the emotional cost has sunk in, and the story is complete. Now what? Before your thriller reaches readers—whether through traditional publishers, self-publishing platforms, or even agents—it needs to look, feel, and *read* like a finished product. This is the phase where presentation meets precision. Where formatting, polishing, and final prep make all the difference.

You don't want your espionage masterpiece to feel like a rough draft. You want it to feel like a classified dossier—crisp, structured, and ready for deployment.

Let's walk through how to get there.

1. Start with Professional Formatting

Your thriller needs to follow industry-standard formatting if you're submitting to agents or publishers, and it needs to look sleek and readable if you're self-publishing. Start by choosing your format path:

- **Manuscript Format** (for agents/publishers):
  - Times New Roman, 12 pt
  - Double-spaced
  - One-inch margins
  - Indented paragraphs, no extra line between them
  - A header with your name, book title, and page number
- **Self-Publishing Format** (for Kindle, paperback, etc.):
  - Use tools like **Vellum**, **Atticus**, or **Reedsy Book Editor**
  - Choose a professional serif font for body text (Garamond, Georgia)
  - Pay attention to justification, line spacing, and clean breaks between chapters
  - Add front matter (title page, copyright, dedication) and back matter (acknowledgments, author bio, teaser for the next book)

If you're unsure, let ChatGPT help:

"Create a checklist for formatting a thriller novel manuscript for agent submission."

Or

"Help me structure my ebook layout for Kindle Direct Publishing, with a professional thriller tone."

2. Final Polish: Line-Level Perfection

At this point, you've revised and AI-assisted your way through major structural edits. Now you're looking for polish. This means:

- Removing passive voice unless it's intentional
- Tightening up long, winding sentences

- Eliminating unnecessary adverbs and filler words
- Ensuring dialogue tags are clean and purposeful
- Cutting repetition or internal monologue that slows momentum

Ask ChatGPT to do spot-checks:

"Polish this paragraph for clarity and pacing in a political thriller tone."

Or

"Rewrite this dialogue exchange to sound more natural and tense between two intelligence officers."

Even better, paste one page at a time and say:

"Edit this like a copyeditor preparing a fast-paced thriller for publication."

The AI won't replace a professional editor, but it can bring your work *very* close to final draft quality—fast.

3. Consistency Check: Names, Locations, Dates, and Tech

Thrillers are complex. You've got operations spanning continents, fake identities, layered backstories, and tech systems that matter. It's easy for small details to shift.

Do a pass specifically for:

- Character name spellings and aliases
- Timeline consistency (do events flow logically over time?)
- Repeated or conflicting technology details (e.g., a phone being both off and traceable)
- Locations: spelling, layout, and logic (especially if based on real cities)

ChatGPT can help spot-check for continuity:

"Did I use consistent naming and background for the antagonist throughout this plot summary?"

Or generate summaries you can cross-reference:

"Summarize all appearances and characteristics of my protagonist from the following pages."

4. Your Book's "Surface": Title, Cover, and Description

Now it's time to think like a reader. Your book needs to *look* like a thriller. It starts with a strong, memorable title—short, sharp, thematic. ChatGPT is ideal for brainstorming:

"Give me a list of tense, one-to-three-word titles for a political thriller about leaked government secrets."

Once you have your title, you'll need:

- A **subtitle** if needed (e.g., *A Jack Mercer Spy Thriller*)
- A **tagline** (optional but punchy: *Truth has a kill switch.*)
- A **cover** that communicates genre (bold fonts, shadows, global backdrops, lone figures, government seals,

drones, cities)

- A **book description/blurb** that hooks in 150–250 words. Ask:
  "Write a back cover blurb for a fast-paced espionage thriller about a rogue analyst uncovering a state-sponsored assassination plot."

Pair this with a professional-looking cover, whether via Canva, MidJourney + Photoshop, or a hired designer.

5. Publishing Path Prep: Know Your Route

If submitting traditionally:

- Prepare a **query letter**: Ask ChatGPT for help:
  "Write a compelling query letter for a 90,000-word political thriller in the style of John le Carré meets Jason Bourne."
- Prepare a **synopsis**: 1–2 pages, summarizing all major plot points (including the ending)

If self-publishing:

- Set up accounts on platforms like Amazon KDP, Kobo, Draft2Digital, IngramSpark
- Upload your formatted ebook and paperback versions
- Price your book strategically—$2.99–$4.99 is standard for debut indie thrillers
- Choose categories and keywords carefully (*Thrillers > Political, Espionage, Conspiracies*)

Use ChatGPT to help brainstorm keywords:

"Give me keyword suggestions for a thriller involving deep state conspiracy, rogue agents, and global surveillance."

6. The Final Step: The First Impression

Before you hit publish or submit to agents, do a final read-through. Read aloud. Listen to the rhythm. Watch for stumbles. Even a perfect sentence can feel flat if it doesn't *sound* right. Use text-to-speech tools or even ask ChatGPT to evaluate the tone:

"Does this chapter opening have the right balance of tension and intrigue?"

You're not looking for perfection.

You're looking for *clarity, confidence, and control.*

A thriller should never feel hesitant. It should pulse, whisper, explode, and linger.

And now—with formatting clean, prose sharp, and cover loaded—you're ready to release your story into the wild.

One Day, One Book – Planning Your Next Political or Spy Thriller

You did it. You wrote a high-stakes political or espionage thriller packed with secrets, betrayals, code names, backchannels, and moral landmines. Whether it took you a month or you pushed through it in a single 24-hour sprint, the structure is now yours. And the next time you sit down to write, you'll be faster, sharper, and more dangerous with the page.

Because once you've written one political thriller, the real mission becomes this: *how to write another*. And possibly, how to do it in just one day—with a little help from your most loyal field operative: ChatGPT.

This final chapter is your blueprint. It's not just about writing fast. It's about writing **strategically**. With focus. With intention. With the structure, characters, and suspense already locked in before you even hit the keyboard.

Here's how you can go from zero to fully drafted thriller in 24 hours.

Hour 1: Define the Core Threat

Every political or spy thriller begins with a spark. A data leak. A mysterious death. A policy reversal. A diplomatic lie. That spark should feel small, but crack open into something massive.

Ask ChatGPT: *"Give me 10 inciting incidents for a modern political thriller involving global espionage, cyber warfare, and whistle-blowers."*

Pick one that excites you. Don't overthink it. Choose the idea that feels like it's already unraveling behind your eyes.

Then ask: *"Summarize a political thriller plot in three acts based on [your chosen idea]."*

This gives you your structure—your bones.

Hour 2–3: Build the Cast

Start with your protagonist. They must be in the system—or *recently removed from it*. An intelligence analyst. A disgraced operative. A foreign asset. Build someone with skills, scars, and a blind spot.

Ask: *"Create a character profile for a former CIA cyber analyst forced to go rogue after discovering surveillance on American citizens."*

Then, create your antagonist—who doesn't think they're the bad guy. Maybe a politician protecting "stability," or an elite spy eliminating threats to the illusion of democracy.

Add 3–5 support characters:

- An insider who helps
- A friend who betrays
- A journalist, hacker, diplomat, or mole

Use prompts like: *"List five supporting characters for a thriller about a covert blackmail network inside the UN."*

Hour 4–5: Outline the Scenes

Now, bullet out 20–30 scenes. Keep them short and high-impact. Think: chase, leak, ambush, debate, revelation, betrayal, breach, standoff.

Ask: *"Create a 30-scene outline for a fast-paced spy thriller about a deep-cover operation gone wrong."*

Break the outline into three acts. Highlight 3 big twists. Your midpoint should be explosive. Your finale should cost something emotional, not just physical.

Hour 6–12: Write Act One

This is the engine start. Set the tone. Establish the threat. Introduce the spy world. End on a hook that flips everything.

Let ChatGPT help with pace: *"Write the opening scene of a political thriller set in an embassy on lockdown."*

Swap back and forth between you writing and the AI supporting. If you get stuck, ask: *"Describe a tense surveillance scene from the POV of a field agent who suspects a mole."*

Write fast. Don't edit yet. Stay in motion.

Hour 13–18: Write Act Two

This is where the chase begins, the clues get deeper, and trust disintegrates. You'll write key set pieces: double-crosses, hacking sequences, eavesdropped calls, maybe a black site interrogation.

Ask: *"Generate tense dialogue between a whistle-blower and their former mentor who may be working for the other side."*

Keep the tension tight. Insert moments of silence, betrayal, moral questioning. Let the protagonist lose control. Raise the stakes with each scene.

By the end of Act Two, they should be at their lowest—exposed, isolated, or betrayed.

Hour 19–22: Write Act Three

Now it's a race against time. Use a countdown device. A leak is imminent. A hit is planned. An election is about to be rigged. Bring the antagonist and protagonist face to face—not for a shootout, but a *revelation*.

Ask: *"Write a climactic scene where a rogue spy confronts their old commander in a private briefing room, knowing the room is bugged."*

End with cost. The hero wins, but something is broken. Trust. Identity. A relationship. Leave a whisper of something still watching.

Hour 23: Rewrite Key Beats

Skim the whole thing. Tighten transitions. Fix clunky dialogue. Use ChatGPT as a surgical tool:

"Rewrite this scene to sound sharper, colder, more espionage-driven."

"Make this paragraph more clipped and tactical—like a Le Carré operative watching a dead drop go bad."

Hour 24: Title, Blurb, Package

Ask ChatGPT: *"Suggest 10 thriller titles for a book about AI surveillance and political cover-ups."*

Then:

"Write a 200-word back cover blurb for a political thriller about a burned spy unearthing a secret drone war."

Drop your manuscript into a formatted template or upload it to a tool like Reedsy or Atticus.

And when it's ready?

Hit "publish."

Not because it's perfect.

But because it's ready to *start the next story*.

Because in this genre, the end is never the end.

It's just the next operation waiting to be greenlit.

And you? You now have the system, the tools, and the mindset to write your next thriller—in one day or one night—whenever the shadows start whispering again.

Examples of Prompts for Spy Thriller Story Design and Structure

Writing a compelling spy thriller is like assembling a covert operation. Every element—your characters, the plot, the setting, the stakes—needs to click together like a cold, metallic mechanism ready to fire. And if you're writing with AI, you can design and structure your story faster and more effectively by learning how to ask the right questions. This chapter gives you a tactical toolkit of *story design and structure prompts*—tested, refined, and field-ready—to help you build intricate plots, morally complex characters, and heart-pounding twists using ChatGPT or your preferred AI collaborator.

Let's break it down into categories:

A. Foundational Plot and Structure Prompts

These prompts help you build your spy thriller from the ground up:

- *"Give me a three-act structure for a spy thriller about a deep-cover operative who discovers their agency has been compromised."*
- *"Outline a fast-paced political thriller where a rookie intelligence analyst stumbles across evidence of an international coup."*
- *"Create a plot arc for a story where the hero is framed for treason and must unravel the conspiracy while being hunted."*
- *"What are five possible inciting incidents for a modern espionage story involving a global surveillance AI?"*
- *"Break down a spy thriller plot into 25 scenes, including major twists, reveals, and reversals."*

B. Protagonist-Centered Story Design Prompts

These prompts develop your lead spy's journey, emotionally and structurally:

- *"Design a spy thriller where the protagonist begins as a loyal operative and becomes a rogue whistle-blower."*
- *"Describe a protagonist arc for a disillusioned agent forced to protect someone they once betrayed."*
- *"Create a hero's journey structure for a field operative caught between loyalty and truth."*
- *"List five internal conflicts a spy might face while pretending to be someone else for months."*
- *"Write the character arc beats of a spy who must team up with their former handler-turned-enemy."*

C. Antagonist and Opposition Structure Prompts

The spy thriller thrives on layered, powerful, intelligent antagonists. Use these prompts to build them:

- *"Build a plot around a political powerbroker who uses an intelligence agency to orchestrate a global incident."*
- *"Give me five antagonist types for a spy thriller who are not obvious villains but believe they're protecting the greater good."*
- *"Design a final confrontation scene between a spy and a manipulative ex-mentor who orchestrated the whole conspiracy."*
- *"Outline a plot where the real antagonist isn't revealed until the third act twist."*

D. Twists, Turns, and Structural Complexity Prompts

These prompts inject spy-level complexity and unpredictability into your story's architecture:

- *"List five third-act twists for a spy thriller that reframe everything the reader has seen."*
- *"How can I structure a spy thriller where the protagonist is unknowingly being manipulated by both sides?"*
- *"What are effective midpoint reversals in espionage thrillers that change the protagonist's mission?"*
- *"Write a story outline for a thriller that plays with dual timelines—past and present operations merging into one climax."*
- *"Describe a nested conspiracy plot where the spy's mission is a decoy for a hidden agenda."*

E. Genre-Specific World-Building Structure Prompts

Sometimes the structure of the thriller shifts based on setting, tone, or subgenre. Try:

- *"Outline a Cold War-era spy thriller set in Berlin, using real historical events as plot beats."*
- *"Create a structure for a near-future spy thriller where cyber warfare is the main form of espionage."*
- *"Give me a plot outline for an international thriller that jumps between four cities and multiple intelligence agencies."*
- *"How would you structure a spy thriller with a noir tone and unreliable narrator?"*

F. Opening and Ending Structure Prompts

Start and end your story with impact using these targeted prompts:

- *"Write three opening scenes for a spy thriller that drop the reader straight into the mission without confusion."*
- *"How can I structure a story so that the final twist is foreshadowed but still shocking?"*
- *"Describe different ways a spy thriller can end with ambiguity, leaving the reader unsettled."*
- *"Outline a story structure where the ending loops back to the opening scene but with completely new meaning."*

G. Hybrid Story Structure Prompts

For thrillers that blend genres or character dynamics:

- *"Combine a spy thriller with a courtroom drama—what's the best way to structure the overlap?"*
- *"How would you structure a romantic subplot into a high-stakes espionage story without slowing down the pace?"*
- *"Create a dual-protagonist spy thriller structure with one character in the field and one in command."*

Final Tip

Always follow up with a refining prompt like:

- *"Now restructure it with higher stakes in Act Two and a more personal motivation for the hero."*
- *"Add emotional beats and moral dilemmas to each act."*

That's how you turn a good structural outline into a *great* one.

Examples of Prompts for Designing Compelling Characters in Spy Thrillers

In a spy thriller, the plot twists will keep the reader hooked, but it's the **characters** who leave a lasting impression. You're not just writing operatives and informants—you're building liars who believe in something, killers with regrets, and patriots who've stopped trusting the flags they serve. The best spy thriller characters are walking contradictions: dangerous, wounded, brilliant, and compromised.

This chapter gives you a field-ready collection of **prompts specifically designed to help you use ChatGPT** (or any AI assistant) to craft multi-dimensional protagonists, antagonists, allies, and wildcards who live in the shadows, chase secrets, and hold onto just enough of their soul to get the job done.

Let's organize these prompts by role and psychological depth.

A. Building a Complex Protagonist

Your main character must be more than "a spy on a mission." They need a worldview, a weakness, and a past that haunts every decision they make. Try:

- *"Create a character profile for a disillusioned former CIA agent pulled back into the field when a former teammate goes rogue."*
- *"Give me a protagonist who has spent years undercover and no longer remembers who they really are."*
- *"Write a psychological profile of a spy who still believes in the mission, but no longer trusts the agency."*
- *"List five emotional wounds or regrets that might drive a spy to sabotage their own operation."*
- *"Describe the internal arc of a protagonist who starts as a patriot and ends as a whistle-blower."*

B. Designing a Memorable Antagonist

Spy thriller villains should be more than caricatures. They often see themselves as protectors of order—or the only one willing to do what's necessary. Build yours with:

- *"Create a morally complex antagonist who believes destabilizing democracy will actually save the world."*
- *"Describe a former operative who now runs a private intelligence empire and controls more secrets than most governments."*
- *"Write the backstory of an intelligence chief who faked their own death to manipulate events behind the scenes."*
- *"What kind of villain would consider mass surveillance a moral imperative for peace?"*
- *"Give me a villain whose ideological belief system mirrors the hero's, but has diverged in execution."*

C. Crafting Allies and Supporting Characters

In spy thrillers, no one is ever just what they seem. Allies may betray, traitors may redeem, and everyone carries hidden motives. For strong secondary characters, ask:

- *"Create a handler who's also hiding a secret from the agent they manage."*
- *"Give me a character who poses as a low-level analyst but is actually a double agent feeding both sides."*
- *"Design a former lover turned reluctant asset with access to a high-ranking official."*
- *"Write a profile of a burned informant living off-grid, who still holds the key to a decades-old operation."*
- *"Give me three wildcard characters who could serve as either allies or enemies depending on what's revealed."*

D. Exploring Internal Conflict and Moral Ambiguity

Characters in spy thrillers often live in ethical gray zones. These prompts help reveal their hidden layers:

- *"What are five moral compromises a spy might make that will later come back to haunt them?"*
- *"Describe the internal monologue of a spy who has to eliminate someone they once trained."*
- *"Create a scene where a spy realizes their entire career has served a lie."*
- *"List psychological side effects of long-term undercover operations on a field agent's relationships and identity."*
- *"Write a private journal entry for a spy who no longer knows who they're loyal to."*

E. Voice, Dialogue, and Interaction

Give your characters distinct voices and layered relationships with dialogue prompts like:

- *"Write a terse conversation between a field agent and their handler where they both know something is wrong but won't say it."*
- *"Create a dialogue between two former lovers who are now on opposite sides of an international operation."*
- *"Write a tense exchange where a spy confronts their mentor about a mission that went sideways ten years ago."*
- *"Craft banter between two intelligence officers who suspect each other of being moles but have to work together."*
- *"Generate three-character dialogues involving a spy, their unwitting contact, and an eavesdropping third party."*

F. Character-Driven Plot Twists

You can use character prompts to build twisty narrative turns:

- *"Describe a character who betrays the team for a reason that makes emotional sense to the reader."*
- *"What secret could a protagonist discover about their own family that rewrites the purpose of their mission?"*
- *"Create a twist where the antagonist is revealed to have been protecting the hero all along—for personal reasons."*

G. Emotionally-Driven Character Arcs

Because espionage is often soul-crushing, spy characters must *evolve or erode*. Ask:

- *"Write the arc of a spy who starts off emotionally detached but is forced to care when someone they're protecting reminds them of their child."*

- *"Describe a redemptive arc for a field operative haunted by collateral damage from a past mission."*
- *"Give me an emotional breakdown moment for a spy who's had to betray too many people they loved."*

Final Tactical Tips

When designing your characters with ChatGPT:

- Follow up your prompt with *refinements* like: *"Now give them a secret that would ruin them if revealed."*
  "Add a personal ritual they use to stay in control."
  "Show how their trauma affects their ability to trust others in dialogue."
- Don't just think in terms of "heroes" and "villains." Everyone's lying. Everyone's scared. Everyone's trying to stay ahead of a system they no longer understand.

In the next chapter, we'll build entire **worlds** to hold these characters—covering safe houses, black sites, political capitals, war zones, backrooms, and tech-rich battlegrounds where surveillance never sleeps.

Because the character might be unforgettable—but the world they vanish into has to be, too.

Examples of Prompts for World Building in Spy Thrillers

In a spy thriller, the world isn't just scenery—it's an ever-shifting battlefield. You're not just building a city or a country. You're constructing networks of surveillance, layers of political corruption, backchannel negotiations, safe houses with secret compartments, and corridors of power where smiling diplomats plan silent wars. Every location is a trap. Every institution is a mask. And every system, no matter how secure, has a flaw.

World-building for spy thrillers isn't about elaborate fantasy kingdoms—it's about crafting a **hyper-real, layered, deceptive world** where characters walk on eggshells and truth is weaponized.

In this chapter, we'll break down **great prompts for using ChatGPT** to build rich, believable, and suspense-filled environments—from global networks to shadowy backrooms and tech systems that feel terrifyingly real.

A. Global Scope and Geopolitical Tension

A spy thriller thrives on global stakes. Use prompts like:

- *"List 10 real or fictional global hotspots where a spy thriller could take place—each with unique political tension."*
- *"Create a geopolitical scenario where an Eastern European country becomes the focus of a cyber-espionage war."*
- *"Describe the diplomatic fallout of an assassination inside a UN conference hall."*
- *"Build a fictional micro-nation created for espionage purposes, complete with a fake economy and passport system."*
- *"What are five current international flashpoints that could serve as the backdrop for an espionage conspiracy?"*

B. Intelligence Agencies and Black Ops Networks

Organizations are as much a part of your world as geography. Design them with:

- *"Create a fictional intelligence agency operating inside a corrupt government. Give it structure, leadership, and operational tactics."*
- *"Describe a secret multinational black-ops alliance between five intelligence agencies with different agendas."*
- *"Give me the internal hierarchy of a private intelligence contractor that sells secrets to the highest bidder."*
- *"List ways a spy agency might cover up its own existence while still executing operations globally."*
- *"Invent a covert AI-driven signals intelligence unit that operates outside any known jurisdiction."*

C. Safe Houses, Black Sites, and Surveillance Environments

Ground your scenes in places that radiate paranoia:

- *"Describe a safe house in rural France outfitted with hidden weapons, burner phones, and an emergency tunnel."*
- *"Build a high-security black site in the Arctic Circle where detainees are interrogated off-grid."*
- *"Give me five surveillance-heavy public spaces that would be perfect for a covert exchange of intel."*
- *"Write the layout of a luxury penthouse secretly built for espionage surveillance in a foreign embassy."*
- *"What defensive measures would a seasoned spy install in their personal residence to detect infiltration?"*

D. CITIES, STREETS, and Spy Capitals

Create immersive urban worlds full of secrets and shadows:

- *"Design the espionage underworld of Berlin, where spies from six countries meet in abandoned metro tunnels."*
- *"Map out a covert spy network operating within Hong Kong's financial sector."*
- *"Describe the layers of intelligence activity happening during a political summit in Geneva."*
- *"Create a fictional Eastern European capital that is a front for illegal weapons testing and data laundering."*
- *"What would a spy see walking through a city like Istanbul during a politically charged protest?"*

E. Technology, Surveillance, and Cyber Infrastructure

Modern spy thrillers need worlds wired for control, leaks, and manipulation:

- *"Describe a national surveillance grid that tracks civilians through facial recognition, payment systems, and mobile metadata."*
- *"Invent a next-gen hacking tool that can extract encrypted files from any offline device within 30 feet."*
- *"Outline a secret communication network used by deep-cover operatives in authoritarian states."*
- *"What security weaknesses might exist in a government-backed social media app?"*
- *"Build a fictional black-market server farm where global secrets are stored and auctioned to intelligence agencies."*

F. Institutions and Political Power Structures

Spy thrillers often intersect with government, business, media, and criminal institutions. Try:

- *"Create a fictional think tank used as cover for state-sponsored psychological operations."*
- *"Describe a multinational energy corporation that funds intelligence operations for access to foreign markets."*
- *"Invent a senator's inner circle—including aides, security, donors—each with their own secrets and agendas."*
- *"What kind of fictional news outlet would subtly spread propaganda for an intelligence agency?"*
- *"Design a diplomatic event where every attendee has a hidden motive—and half are spies."*

G. Cultural Tension, Language Barriers, and Local Realism

Add richness to your world with culturally specific detail:

- *"Describe how a covert agent might navigate cultural taboos while trying to gather intel in Tehran."*
- *"Write a scene where a spy uses regional slang to gain the trust of a black-market informant in Lagos."*
- *"How could a language barrier compromise a surveillance op in rural China?"*
- *"List customs or social signals a spy must understand to avoid suspicion while operating in Cairo."*
- *"Design a coded ritual or religious event used to mask intelligence activity in a politically unstable region."*

H. Hidden Architecture and Symbolism

Some of the best thriller moments happen in secret rooms, passages, or misused spaces:

- *"Describe a forgotten Cold War bunker repurposed for a modern operation in the Swiss Alps."*
- *"Create a luxury hotel built with hidden surveillance architecture used by multiple agencies."*

- *"List five ways ancient architecture (cathedrals, catacombs, castles) could be used to hide modern espionage tools."*
- *"Write about a national museum with a secret sub-basement used for prisoner exchanges."*

Final Prompting Tips

Once you generate your world:

- Use follow-ups to deepen the layers:
  "Who really controls this city behind the scenes?"
  "What's the one flaw in this surveillance system?"
  "What event from the past still echoes in this location today?"
- Let ChatGPT simulate documents:
  "Write a redacted intelligence report about an operation that failed in this city."
- Combine world-building with character development:
  "How does this environment shape the mindset of a local informant who's been burned before?"

Spy thrillers aren't just set in places. They *hide in them.*

In the next chapter, we'll turn to **idea generation for full stories**—how to use AI prompts to brainstorm gripping plots, reverse-engineer twists, and craft conspiracies so complex and chilling, they just might be true.

Examples of Good Prompts for Spy Thriller Story Ideas

A great spy thriller begins with an idea that feels dangerous. It's not just a story—it's a secret you're letting the reader uncover. Whether it's a missing agent, a whistle-blower on the run, or a government program no one is supposed to know about, the best spy thriller ideas are built on tension, betrayal, and consequences that stretch across borders.

With ChatGPT, you can go from a vague concept to a sharp, high-stakes idea in minutes—if you know how to prompt it. This chapter offers a toolbox of **story idea prompts**, designed specifically for the world of spy thrillers. Use them to generate plots that feel timely, terrifying, and impossible to put down.

A. Single-Line Story Concept Prompts

Quick prompts to generate big-picture thriller ideas:

- *"Give me 10 spy thriller story ideas involving rogue agents, secret assassinations, and surveillance gone wrong."*
- *"What's a gripping story premise for a thriller where the CIA and MI6 are secretly at war with each other?"*
- *"Generate a plot idea for a political thriller involving a deep-cover operative embedded in a foreign parliament."*
- *"Give me a spy thriller idea inspired by real Cold War tactics, reimagined in a modern cyberwar setting."*
- *"Create a story hook involving a sleeper agent who wakes up and doesn't know which country they were working for."*

B. Twist-Based Prompts

Start with the twist and build the story around it:

- *"What's a spy thriller idea where the protagonist discovers they've been the decoy all along?"*
- *"Create a thriller where the villain is revealed to be the protagonist's missing sibling working for an enemy agency."*
- *"Describe a story where the leaked intel turns out to be planted by the protagonist's own agency to flush out a mole."*
- *"Give me an espionage story idea where the 'dead drop' actually contains evidence that will ruin the hero's reputation."*
- *"Write a spy thriller concept with a third-act twist revealing the entire mission was staged for political theater."*

C. Real-World Inspired Prompts

Grounded thrillers feel like they could happen tomorrow:

- *"Give me a spy thriller idea based on tensions between NATO countries and a mysterious satellite malfunction."*
- *"What's a spy story that explores foreign influence over elections through deepfake technology?"*
- *"Generate a story idea involving a whistle-blower revealing a drone program that targets citizens abroad."*
- *"Write a spy thriller pitch where a journalist uncovers a decades-old CIA operation still active today."*
- *"Describe a plot set in post-Brexit Europe where old alliances are weaponized against each other by a rogue nation."*

D. CHARACTER-DRIVEN Prompts

Start with the operative and let the story follow:

- *"Describe a spy thriller where the protagonist is a retired assassin pulled back in after a copycat killer resurfaces."*
- *"Give me a story where a young surveillance analyst realizes they're watching someone they were never meant to find."*
- *"What's a plot idea where a diplomat's child secretly feeds intel to a foreign government?"*
- *"Create a thriller centered on a burned operative trying to prove they were framed before they're eliminated."*
- *"Outline a story where an undercover agent is slowly being turned by the very people they're meant to betray."*

E. Setting-Based Prompts

Let the location inspire the conspiracy:

- *"Give me a spy thriller story set entirely inside a single secure embassy during a lockdown."*
- *"Create a story idea for a spy thriller that takes place across five cities in 72 hours."*
- *"What's a spy plot set in Antarctica, where a research base is actually a surveillance hub?"*
- *"Describe a story set during a G20 summit, where a hit is planned under the cover of diplomacy."*
- *"Generate an espionage story that uses a remote Pacific island as a Cold War-era intelligence vault."*

F. Tech and AI-Based Story Prompts

Spy thrillers are evolving—so should your plots:

- *"What's a spy thriller story idea involving an AI system trained to detect national threats but begins targeting its own creators?"*
- *"Create a plot where a hacker leaks intelligence about a surveillance program that doesn't officially exist."*
- *"Give me a story idea involving a rogue algorithm that starts predicting assassinations before they happen."*
- *"Describe a thriller where the protagonist uses facial recognition systems to trace an agent who's been erased from history."*
- *"Generate a modern espionage plot around a viral app secretly gathering psychological profiles for a foreign agency."*

G. High-Concept and Genre-Bending Prompts

For stories that blend styles and defy expectations:

- *"Create a spy thriller with elements of noir, where the protagonist is investigating their own memories."*
- *"What's a thriller story that combines espionage with courtroom drama—where the trial is being watched by global spy agencies?"*
- *"Describe a spy thriller with horror undertones, involving an abandoned government experiment coming back online."*
- *"Give me a concept for a spy thriller told from the POV of a civilian caught in an operation without realizing it."*
- *"Write a story concept where a group of retired spies are pulled back into service when their old mission is declassified."*

Final Tactical Tip

Once you get a raw idea, **refine it** with AI:

- *"Expand this concept into a 10-chapter outline with twists, key characters, and global stakes."*
- *"Who are the main players in this story, and how do their loyalties shift by the end?"*
- *"What moral conflict can I build into this idea to deepen the emotional arc?"*

In the next chapter, we'll dive into **your one-day writing game plan**—a complete workflow that takes these ideas, plugs them into a proven structure, and gets you from blank page to full draft in just 24 hours.

Because the world of espionage never sleeps—and neither should your storytelling.

Your One-Day Spy Thriller Writing Game Plan

So, you're ready to write a full-blown spy thriller in one day. Not an outline. Not a few cool scenes. A complete, pulse-pounding, morally twisted, plot-twisting, character-driven espionage story that feels like a movie in your reader's hands. Sound impossible? Not with the right system—and the right partner.

This chapter is your **tactical operation plan**, broken down into manageable phases that take you from idea to published draft in 24 hours using ChatGPT and some good old-fashioned writer discipline. This isn't about rushing through junk—it's about writing fast, focused, and smart.

Let's begin your one-day intelligence mission.

Mission Briefing: Your Objective

Write and publish a 20,000 to 30,000-word spy thriller novella in 24 hours using ChatGPT as your co-writer. This will be a standalone story or a pilot episode for a series.

Your tone: Tense, smart, morally gray.

Your pace: Fast. Scene to scene. Dialogue-heavy.

Your result: A tightly structured, plot-driven thriller ready for Self-Publishing or other platforms.

Hour 1: Story Intel – Generate Your Core Concept

Start with a single idea. One event. One breach. One secret.

Ask ChatGPT:

- *"Give me 10 high-stakes spy thriller story ideas involving betrayal inside an intelligence agency."*

Choose the one that hits you hardest. Refine it:

- *"Expand this into a three-act structure with a twist in the second act and a morally ambiguous ending."*

Then ask:

- *"Give me five compelling characters for this plot, including one double agent."*

Now you've got your concept, act structure, and core cast.

Hour 2: Chapter Breakdown and Timeline

Ask ChatGPT to:

- *"Turn this plot into a 12-chapter outline with escalating tension and reveals in each chapter."*

Then prompt:

- *"Add short descriptions to each chapter that show setting, character, and purpose."*

You now have your scene map. You're not writing blind—you're executing a plan.

Hour 3–5: Write Act One (Chapters 1–4)

Use ChatGPT to help write opening scenes:

- *"Write the opening chapter where the protagonist receives a mysterious message from a presumed-dead agent."*

Go paragraph by paragraph. Feed AI your drafts and ask:

- *"Punch up this dialogue to sound like real spy banter."*

Alternate between writing your own scenes and letting AI fill gaps. Keep the pacing brisk and tight.

Hour 6–10: Write Act Two (Chapters 5–9)

This is the bulk of the thriller. Here, the chase begins. The betrayal hits. The mole is exposed—or is it a setup?

Ask:

- *"Write a scene where the protagonist realizes they're being followed, but the pursuer might be a friend."*
- *"Create a twist scene where the supposed villain saves the hero, forcing an uneasy alliance."*

Let ChatGPT suggest high-tension locations:

- *"Give me five unique international settings for a clandestine exchange during a protest."*

Keep action clean, motives hidden, dialogue meaningful.

Hour 11–13: Write Act Three (Chapters 10–12)

You're at the climax now. The conspiracy is revealed. The final betrayal hits. The protagonist must make a devastating choice.

Ask:

- *"Write a final confrontation between a rogue agent and their former mentor, with emotional fallout and deadly consequences."*

Then:

- *"Craft an ending that leaves room for a sequel but still gives closure."*

Once the final scene lands, breathe. You've drafted your novella.

Hour 14–16: Rapid Editing Pass

Now ask ChatGPT to help you line-edit fast:

- *"Edit this chapter for grammar, pacing, and dialogue realism."*
- *"Cut filler words and passive voice from this scene."*
- *"Make this paragraph read like a John le Carré internal monologue."*

Go chapter by chapter. Don't obsess—polish for clarity, consistency, and tone.

Hour 17–18: Title, Cover, and Blurb

Ask:

- *"Suggest 10 sharp titles for a spy thriller about betrayal inside the NSA."*

Then:

- *"Write a back-cover blurb in the tone of a political espionage thriller."*

Now generate your cover image. Use MidJourney, Canva, or ask ChatGPT:

- *"Create an image prompt for a spy thriller book cover—dark city, silhouette, global map overlay, no text."*

Upload that image. You're now ready for packaging.

Hour 19–21: Formatting for Publication

Use Reedsy Book Editor, Atticus, Vellum, Draft2Digital or Kindle Create. Add:

- Front matter (Title Page, Copyright, Dedication)
- Chapters, with clean breaks
- Back matter (Acknowledgments, Bio, Link to next book or series teaser)

Export to ePub, PDF, and KDP formats.

Hour 22: KDP Upload or Draft Saving

Go to https://draft2digital.com

or kdp.amazon.com[1]

Upload your manuscript and cover

- Insert title, blurb, and keywords (use ChatGPT for help:
  "Give me 7 keywords for a spy thriller involving surveillance and rogue agents.")
- Set pricing and preview

---

1. https://kdp.amazon.com/

You don't have to hit publish today—but you *can*.

Alternatively, save everything as a finished draft for a soft launch or serial release.

Hour 23–24: Reflect, Reuse, Reload

Ask ChatGPT to summarize what you wrote:

- *"Summarize the plot of this book in 200 words."*
- *"Describe this protagonist's emotional arc."*

Now ask:

- *"How can I expand this into a trilogy?"*
- *"Suggest a second book that raises the stakes but keeps the same tone."*

You're not just done—you've set the foundation for your **next mission**.

Final Debrief

You just wrote a complete spy thriller in one day.

You now have:

- A tight, structured novella
- A professional-looking book package
- A launch-ready product
- The framework for a series
- And a system you can reuse tomorrow

Because storytelling at this level isn't about speed—it's about *precision*.

One day. One thriller. One hell of a story. Now exfil safely. You've earned it.

I hope you found inspiration within these pages. If you liked this book, please leave a review where you bought it. Thank you from the author.

About the Author

Andrew Parry is a writer and filmmaker with a profound love for film, particularly the genre of science fiction. His passion for the limitless possibilities of sci-fi drives both his storytelling and his creative vision. For Andrew, science fiction is more than just a genre—it's a way to explore the boundaries of human imagination, the future of technology, and the mysteries of the universe. Through his writing and filmmaking, Andrew seeks to create narratives that transport audiences to worlds filled with awe, wonder, and the thrill of discovery.

Read more at https://lonetrail.blog.

www.ingramcontent.com/pod-product-compliance
Lightning Source LLC
LaVergne TN
LVHW082344200926
848481LV00012B/3449